Ready and Waiting

Introduction

When I told my friends and colleagues that I was writing a slow cooker cookbook, the reactions were divided right down the middle. Half of them said that they, like myself, had happily and successfully cooked in a slow cooker for years, and that it was their best friend in the kitchen. Others stated vehemently that they had tried to use a slow cooker years ago, hated it, and either threw it out, stashed it in the darkest corners of the garage, or turned the crockery insert into a planter.

I couldn't figure out why there was such a dramatic difference in opinion, especially when my mouth watered as I remembered some of the fantastic dishes that have come out of my slow cooker: old-fashioned stews, hearty chilis, rib-sticking soups, and zesty pasta sauces. How would I make my Grandma Edith's Persimmon Gingerbread Pudding for Christmas dinner without my slow cooker? Did those slow cooker detractors know that it makes scorch-free Pineapple and Macadamia Chutney and Gingered Apple Butter? Didn't they use the slow cooker on hot summer days to create luscious desserts without turning on the oven, and in the winter to make unbeatable stews?

To help me solve the dilemma, I asked the anti–slow cooker contingent to send me some of their recipes. From the first batch I received, the message was clear: Don't ignore the basic standards of good cooking just because you're cooking with a slow cooker. Here's an example from the kitchen of Mrs. X (the name has been changed to protect the innocent):

Coq au Vin
1 whole chicken, skinned and cut into 8 pieces
3 tablespoons oil
1 onion, chopped

continued

4 cloves garlic

Salt and pepper

2 cups semisweet wine

Handful of mushrooms

2 or 3 potatoes

Throw all the ingredients in the pot. Turn it on. Cook from morning till evening.

What about browning the chicken so the caramelized skin can add flavor and body to the sauce? (Where is the skin?) What about some chicken broth for the sauce? What is semisweet wine? Isn't the sauce thickened? How about some herbs?

I took my friend's recipe and cooked it her way, for eight hours. The chicken was like a squeezed-out sponge, and the potatoes fell apart in a watery, flavorless sauce, studded with sharp-tasting bits of onion.

Then I took the same basic list of ingredients and made coq au vin in the slow cooker my way, using the same principles of good cooking that I always use, whether I'm cooking in a slow cooker or on top of a stove. I browned the chicken (skin on, but removed after cooking) in the oil, then softened the onions and garlic in the same pan to release their flavors. I did add some parsley and thyme, and I used dry red wine instead of "semisweet," but I didn't go overboard when adjusting the recipe's ingredients. I cooked the chicken for six hours, after which time the meat was tender but not overdone. I thickened the cooking liquid, first skimming off the fat, by reducing it on top of the stove. While the ingredients for both recipes cost the same amount of money, my few minutes of extra effort improved the dish immeasurably, beyond just throwing ingredients in the pot.

Ready and Waiting shows cooks how to use the slow cooker. Its best feature is its unique constant cooking temperature. Throughout this book I have adapted favorite recipes that require long, slow simmering. The French have contributed many ragoûts from their cuisine that benefit from cooking slowly and leisurely such as Beef Bourguignon and, yes, Coq au Vin. My grandmother used her bean pot to coax dried beans into wholesome baked beans, and my Sugarbush Beans, among other legume recipes, celebrate this tradition. The slow cooker makes an impressive variety of delectable desserts, from steamed pudding cakes such as Steamed Chocolate-Pecan Pudding to Strawberry-Strawberry Cheesecake.

In addition, if the oven is being used to roast a turkey or bake a cake, the slow cooker can prepare side dishes that take well to long cooking. When you are entertaining, the slow cooker can take some of the pressure off; it keeps dips hot or serves as a punch bowl for beverages that are served warm.

When you just want a simple but satisfying meal, few things hit the spot like a chunky soup, and I've included hearty renditions, such as Jamaican Oxtail Soup and Chinese Chicken Hot Pot. And since dinner will be cooking on the countertop, I've included a few stove top items to go with your slow-cooked entrées, as well as fresh-from-the-oven quick breads and fresh salads.

What Is Slow-Cooked Cuisine?

There are many advantages to using a slow cooker:

· The slow cooker needs virtually no watching or tending while it cooks, allowing the cook to concentrate on other chores or recipes, especially handy when you're trying to cook for a large party.

· The slow cooker allows you to be out of the kitchen for long periods of time—even all day for some recipes.

· The slow cooker tenderizes less expensive, tough cuts of meat, making the best stews possible.

· The slow cooker's lengthy cooking period allows flavors to mingle better than conventional methods.

· The slow cooker makes many dishes, especially those that tend to stick to the bottom of the pan, better than any other appliance, allowing the food to cook for extended periods of time without burning or requiring excessive attention.

· The slow cooker frees you to use the oven and stove for other dishes that are at their best when cooked by those methods. For example, use the slow cooker to prepare side dishes while your holiday entree is in the oven.

There are some misconceptions about what slow cookers can and can't do that require clarification:

The slow cooker, like any other kitchen appliance, does not cook *everything* to perfection. Large cuts of of meat like leg of lamb and boneless prime rib are best when oven-roasted, and to detour from the conventional method of preparation is a waste of time and money. Save the slow cooker for what it does best—stews, chilis, smothered vegetables, and puddings!

Except for chowders and stews, the slow cooker does not cook fish well.

When cooking meat, the slow cooker collects a lot of juices. Because steam rising from the food in a slow cooker does not escape during cooking, these juices become watery and diluted by the steam, and can affect the flavors. To compensate, meats must be browned in a skillet or Dutch oven on top of the stove before they are added to the slow cooker, and the liquid must be reduced after cooking to make sauces. If you follow these two important steps, you can get superior results.

Despite what you may have heard to the contrary, the slow cooker *can* overcook food. Since slow cookers first appeared more than a dozen years ago, meats and poultry have become both leaner and more tender. Try subtracting an hour or so from your old slow cooker recipes to reflect these changes.

Here are answers to some of the most frequently asked questions about slow-cooked cuisine.

How does the slow cooker work?

The slow cooker uses the time-flavored method of cooking foods slowly to enhance their flavor and texture. At the low setting, the temperature is about 200°F, below boiling. The high setting is about 300°F, so the food will simmer and boil. Most slow cookers have a crockery insert because crockery is an excellent insulator and holds the heat in. The slow cooker runs on very little electricity, and it maintains an extremely low, consistent temperature. Do not be tempted to lift the lid and peek into the slow cooker while cooking, as precious steam will escape. Remember, it is the hot air surrounding the ingredients that does the cooking, and lifting the lid, even for a moment, will reduce the air's temperature. If you do remove the lid, add an additional twenty minutes to the recipe to raise the heat back up to its desired temperature. (In recipes where I direct you to stir, this additional time has been figured into the total cooking time.)

Are all slow cookers the same?

No. There are two different kinds of slow cookers. The most common model does nothing but slow-cook. It has a crockery insert and two temperature readings, low and high. On most of these models, the heating element is coiled up the sides of the housing unit, so the heat "surrounds" the insert. This method gives low, even heat and discourages scorching. I prefer this type of slow cooker, as it was designed to do just one job and do it well. This was the original slow-cooker model, and I'm not convinced it has been improved upon. By the way, the term Crockpot is not generic; it's Rival Manufacturing Company's trademarked name for their specific slow cooker, the granddaddy of them all. All of the recipes in this book were tested with the Rival Crockpot.

The other kind of slow cooker is actually a "multi-cooker." Multi-cookers come with adjustable thermostats, so they can be used for other cooking methods, such as deep frying, as well as slow-cooking. To slow-cook in a multi-cooker, set the thermostat at 200°F for low, and 300°F for high. In most multi-cooker models, the heating element is located at the bottom of the housing unit, so the heat is applied only at the bottom of the pot. Some multi-cookers come with a crockery insert to help distribute this bottom-generated heat, but food can still scorch at the bottom where the crockery comes into contact with the element. Be aware of this problem if you cook my recipes in a multi-cooker, and stir the food two or three times during the cooking period to be sure it's not sticking! Add 20 minutes to your recipe every time the lid is lifted. The advantage to a multi-cooker is that if the food hasn't finished cooking when you want it, you can turn the thermostat up as high as you want to complete the job.

How do I cook a recipe in a shorter time than indicated?

To cook a recipe that calls for low temperatures on high, estimate about one hour on high for every two hours on low. However, the times stated in each recipe reflect the temperature that will give the best results. For example, pot roasts will be best if they are slowly simmered, not boiled. As the low setting is 200°F, boiling is avoided. If you cook the pot roast at 300°F, it may be not turn out as well as it would at the lower temperature.

If I want a recipe to take longer than indicated, what do I do?

Purchase a houseware timer at the hardware store. Fill the slow cooker, attach it to the timer, and set it to start NO LONGER THAN TWO HOURS LATER. With poultry dishes, this time is reduced to ONE HOUR. Do not let the cooked food stand for longer than TWO HOURS after it is cooked. For food safety reasons, this method is reliable only when all of the ingredients put into the pot are chilled.

My carrots and potatoes never get done in the slow cooker. What am I doing wrong?

Harder vegetables, like carrots, potatoes, and other root vegetables, should be cut into small pieces no bigger than 1-inch square. Place them on the bottom of the slow cooker so the vegetables begin to cook as soon as the cooking liquid heats. Should you wish to retain the crisp texture of some vegetables in stews, however, cook them separately on the stove and stir them into the stew at the end of the slow-cooking period. Strong-tasting leafy vegetables, such as collard greens and green cabbage, are often parcooked before adding to the slow cooker. Parcooking diminishes the strong flavors that might overpower the other vegetables during the long cooking process, and wilts the vegetables to reduce the amount of space they require in the slow cooker.

An important tip: Scrub potatoes or turnips well with a brush but do not peel; the skin helps them retain their shape and color in the cooking liquid.

My recipes say I can make the gravy right in the slow cooker, but it always tastes watery. How do I make a good sauce from the cooking liquid?

Many old slow-cooker recipes suggest stirring instant tapioca, cornstarch, or flour pastes into the cooking liquid to make gravy. Remember that the cooking liquids are diluted in slow cooking and need to be reduced to intensify their flavors. While each recipe in this book gives exact amounts, here's the basic technique for reducing sauces: In a medium saucepan over low heat, melt butter and whisk in flour to make a roux. (*Roux* is the classic French cooking term for the cooked butter and flour mixture used to thicken sauces.) After skimming the fat from the surface of the cooking liquid, whisk the cooking liquid into the roux and bring the mixture to a simmer. As the sauce cooks for a few minutes and thickens, the excess liquid is boiled away, and the resulting sauce is highly superior to one made with tapioca. I don't know anyone who actually likes the taste or texture of tapioca in gravy.

In some recipes, mostly for soups and chowders, I do stir a cornstarch mixture directly into the slow cooker, as the flavors are more intense in these dishes. In others, I purée the vegetables with the cooking liquid to make a delicious sauce.

How can I remove unwanted fat from my slow-cooker recipes?

Choose lean cuts of meat and trim away as much visible fat as possible. When cooking poultry, cook with the skin on, but remove the skin before serving.

When browning meat or poultry, use a nonstick skillet sprayed lightly with vegetable cooking spray.

Skim the fat from the surface of the cooking liquid before serving. Using a slotted spoon, transfer the meat and vegetables to a serving platter. Pour the cooking liquid into a glass measuring cup, and let stand for about five minutes, until the clear fat rises to the surface of the liquid. Then skim off the fat with a large spoon.

The most efficient method of fat removal is to allow the dish to cool to room temperature, cover and refrigerate it until the fat chills and solidifies on the surface, and then scrape the solidified fat away. (The finished dish can be warmed in either a conventional or a microwave oven or transferred to a large saucepan and reheated over low heat.)

I want to adapt a favorite recipe for the slow cooker. What adjustments should I make?

Meats should always be well trimmed. If the meat isn't lean, it will release its fats into the cooking liquid. Too much fat in your cooking liquid will raise its temperature, and your meat may get overcooked. Browning meats before putting them in the slow cooker helps reduce the fat content. Certain cuts, such as beef and pork ribs and oxtails, are easier to brown in a broiler. Chicken should be browned on the skin side only in a skillet before it goes into the slow cooker.

In choosing a cut of meat for slow-cooked pot roasts, be sure to pick a size that will fit into your slow cooker. Boneless cuts can be cut into pieces that can be layered in the slow cooker if necessary.

Liquids will be diluted as the steam collects under the lid of the slow cooker and drips back down into the cooking liquid. In a stew, for example, I normally acquire at least half a cup of excess water during the cooking period. Reduce the amount of liquid in your traditional recipe by about one-half. Soups generally need no adjustment, but consider the size of your slow cooker: Most hold only about 3½ quarts, so large yield recipes should be reduced accordingly. I prefer to use canned or homemade double-strength chicken or beef broth to be sure I get the proper flavor impact. Adjust the amount of salt in the recipe to balance the amount in the broth. The canned double-strength broths are clearly marked as such, but you may find them mixed in with the soups rather than grouped with the other canned broths. You may certainly use homemade stocks, but be sure they are full-flavored. (See the recipe for Double-Strength Chicken or Beef Stock, page 30, which can be used in regular cooking, too.) One 10½-ounce can of broth equals 1⅓ cups.

If using canned tomatoes, use tomatoes packed in thick tomato purée to get the fullest flavor.

Herbs should be the dried leaf variety, not ground. (This holds true in regular cooking, too, as the ground herbs have a much shorter shelf life.) In slow-cooking, the already-weak flavor of ground herbs would be lost during the long cooking period. If in doubt, season the dish at the end.

Milk products, like natural cheese, do not hold up well during long periods of cooking, so add cheese toward the end of cooking, just to melt. (Slow cooker manufacturers recommend cooking with processed cheese, but I never use it in my cooking, slow-cooked or conventional.) Regular milk will curdle if cooked too long, but you can substitute evaporated milk. In recipes that need a dairy flavor, such as chowders or cream soups, I prefer to stir heavy or sour cream into the cooking liquid just before serving.

Eggs do best in custardlike dishes that are cooked in soufflé dishes or other utensils that are placed *in* the slow cooker, as they may curdle if they come in contact with the warm walls of the crockery insert for too long.

To time an adapted recipe for the slow cooker, estimate three to four hours on low for every hour of conventional cooking. (Estimate about two to two and a half hours on high for each hour.)

What about the different sizes of slow cookers?

There are three basic sizes of slow cooker. The 1-quart model is perfect for cooks who entertain frequently, keeping dips warm for hours. I find this size too small for everyday cooking, and use mine only at parties.

The most popular slow cooker is the 3½-quart model. Most of the recipes in this book were tested in this size, but will also be successful made in a 4-quart model. These two models hold enough food for four to six servings, including up to 3½-pound bone-in roasts. Boneless roasts can be larger, but you will have to cut them into pieces and layer them in the slow cooker. (The exact fit of the meat is based on the size and shape of the roast, not just the weight, so trim a little if necessary.) If you are a dessert lover, note that the 3½-quart model will not hold a standard 2½-quart pudding mold. (I've included plenty of recipes that will fit, however.)

The 5-quart model is best for big families and for recipes that call for large cuts of meat, such as corned beef, or dishes that serve a crowd, or steamed puddings. If you want to adjust a 3½-quart model recipe for the 5-quart size, increase the ingredients by one-half. To use larger roasts than indicated in the 3½-quart recipes, increase the cooking time by one and one half hours per additional pound on low to be sure the meat is tender.

Is slow cooking safe? What about bacteria growth in food that is at room temperature for so long?

Bacteria growth is inhibited at temperatures above 180 degrees. The temperature of the food in a slow cooker reaches this point (and above) in a quick enough period of time that bacteria growth is not a problem.

How do I clean my slow cooker?

The removable crockery insert can be washed in a dishwasher, or in warm, soapy water. Do not run cold water into a hot insert or it may crack. To remove stubborn cooked-on food, simply soak the insert in warm, soapy water. Do not use abrasive cleaners or scouring pads or you will scratch the crockery.

Never immerse the metal housing unit in water! To clean the inside or outside of the unit, *unplug,* spray with liquid household cleaner, and wipe with a damp sponge.

Are there any variables I should know about?

Extreme humidity can affect cooking time. At altitudes higher than 3,500 feet, you may have to cook the foods for longer periods. Sometimes there may be voltage variations, and the slow cooker may get reduced power for a short period of time.

Dips and Appetizers

Appetizers set the mood for a meal or party, whether it's a casual get-together or an elegant soirée. However, the busy cook can often be so caught up in preparing the main course and dessert that the hors d'oeuvre are demoted to a few crackers and some cheese. The slow cooker can help create enticing appetizers that are thankfully easy to make. This chapter features recipes that run the gamut from crunchy munchies like Chinese Bridge Mix to sophisticated first courses like Chicken Liver and Apple Terrine.

It is a relief to have a recipe file full of delicious dips and appetizers that practically cook themselves in the slow cooker. No constant stirring, no peeking in the oven every few minutes to check for scorching, no fretting about overcooking. Many of my favorite appetizer recipes taste better when slow-cooked. The carrots, celery, and cauliflower in the Tarragon Pickled Vegetables slowly soak up the marinade, giving them a fuller flavor than if cooked on the stove. Caponata, which normally takes constant watching to avoid burning, is hassle-free when made in a slow cooker. My pâtés and terrines improve when cooked in the slow cooker, as the low temperature keeps them from shrinking excessively.

Dips have always been popular, but a hot dip is an extra-special way to serve this cocktail party must-have. The 1-quart mini–slow cooker is one of the best friends you can invite to a party. I often start the dip on the stove or in the oven, then transfer it to the slow cooker, where it keeps at perfect serving temperature for hours.

Three of these recipes can even be given as holiday gifts: Christmas Sugared Walnuts, Cajun Pecans, and Tarragon Pickled Vegetables. Pack them in attractive glass jars and decorate with big ribbons.

Caponata

Caponata, the Italian eggplant and vegetable salad, is one of the most versatile appetizers you can have on hand. It will keep for at least a week in the refrigerator and up to a month in the freezer. Serve with slices of French bread. In case of unexpected guests, toss it with cooked pasta for a quick supper.

Makes about 6 cups

The easiest way to pit Mediterranean olives is to simply squeeze the pits out between your fingers. You don't have to be concerned about the appearance of the smashed olives here, since they're going to be chopped anyway.

1. In a large colander, toss the eggplant cubes with 1 teaspoon of the salt. Let stand about 1 hour. Rinse the eggplant cubes well under cold running water and drain.

2. In a 3½-quart slow cooker, layer the vegetables in the following order: eggplant, carrots, celery, onion, zucchini, and garlic. In a medium bowl, combine the tomatoes, water, olive oil, tomato paste, vinegar, sugar, basil, the remaining ½ teaspoon salt, and the crushed pepper. Add to the vegetables, cover, and cook until the vegetables are tender, 6 to 7 hours on low (200°F). During the last hour of cooking, increase the heat to high (300°F) and uncover to evaporate the excess liquid.

3. Cool the caponata to room temperature. Stir in the capers and olives. Cover and refrigerate overnight to allow the flavors to mellow.

4. Bring the caponata to room temperature before serving.

1 medium eggplant (about 1¼ pounds), cut into ¾-inch cubes

1½ teaspoons salt, divided

2 medium carrots, cut into ½-inch-thick rounds

1 medium celery rib, cut into ½-inch-thick slices

1 medium onion, chopped

2 medium zucchini, cut into ½-inch-thick rounds

2 garlic cloves, minced

1 15-ounce can peeled Italian tomatoes, drained and chopped

¼ cup water

2 tablespoons olive oil

2 tablespoons tomato paste

2 tablespoons red wine vinegar

1 tablespoon sugar

1 teaspoon dried basil

¼ teaspoon crushed hot red pepper

2 tablespoons capers

½ cup Mediterranean black olives (such as Calamata), pitted and chopped

Roquefort Cheesecake with Walnut Crust

Not a dessert, this cheesecake is an elegant, savory spread to serve with crisp crackers. Small clusters of red and green grapes make a nice edible garnish.

Makes about 20 servings

1. Generously butter the inside of an 8-inch round springform pan. Press the nuts onto the bottom of the pan.

2. In a medium bowl, using a hand-held electric mixer set at medium-high speed, beat the cream cheese until smooth. Beat in the blue cheese and ½ cup of the sour cream. One at a time, beat in the eggs. Beat in the cornstarch and pepper. Spread the mixture evenly in the prepared pan. Cover tightly with foil.

3. Place a collapsible vegetable steamer or a slow-cooker meat rack in a 5-quart slow cooker. Pour in 2 cups hot water. Place the cheesecake in the slow cooker, cover, and cook until the sides of the cheesecake have risen, 2½ to 3 hours on high (300°F). (Do not cook on low for a longer period of time.) Let the cheesecake stand in the slow cooker until cool enough to handle.

4. Remove the cheesecake and refrigerate, covered, at least 4 hours or up to two days.

5. Run a sharp knife around the inside of the pan to loosen the cheesecake and remove the sides. Spread the top of the cheesecake with the remaining ¼ cup sour cream and sprinkle with the parsley. Serve with crackers.

1½ cups walnut pieces (about 6 ounces), toasted (see page 202) and finely chopped

1 pound cream cheese, well softened

5 ounces blue cheese, preferably Roquefort, well softened

¾ cup sour cream, divided

2 large eggs, at room temperature

1 tablespoon cornstarch

¼ teaspoon freshly ground black pepper

2 tablespoons chopped fresh parsley, for garnish

Crackers

Castroville Artichoke Dip

This is a recipe that has been in my family for ages and one that I never tire of. Serve with toasted baguette slices, crackers, or breadsticks. Now that I serve it in a mini-crockpot, it can be kept at its optimum serving temperature for hours.

Makes 8 to 12 servings

1. Preheat the oven to 325°F. Lightly oil a 1-quart slow-cooker crockery insert.

2. In a medium bowl, combine the artichoke hearts, mozzarella and Parmesan cheeses, mayonnaise, and garlic. Spread evenly in the prepared crockery insert. Sprinkle the top with the bread crumbs and paprika, then drizzle with the oil.

3. Bake until the top is crusty and golden brown, about 30 minutes.

4. Transfer the crockery insert to the slow cooker, set on low (200°F). The slow cooker will keep the dip at proper serving temperature for up to 4 hours.

2 8-ounce jars marinated artichoke hearts, drained and coarsely chopped

1 cup shredded mozzarella cheese (about 4 ounces)

½ cup freshly grated imported Parmesan cheese (about 2 ounces)

½ cup mayonnaise

1 garlic clove, minced

½ cup fresh bread crumbs

½ teaspoon paprika, preferably sweet Hungarian

2 teaspoons olive oil

15

Tarragon Pickled Vegetables

Preparing the vegetables in a slow cooker allows them to soak up the herbed marinade. Serve them as part of an appetizer spread, or as a side dish for Bollito Misto (page 92).

Makes about 2 quarts

1. In a 3½-quart slow cooker, combine the water, vinegar, onion, garlic, salt, tarragon, sugar, and peppercorns. Add the cauliflower, carrots, and celery; stir well. Slow-cook, uncovered, until the vegetables are crisp-tender, about 2 hours on low (200°F).

2. Using a slotted spoon, transfer the vegetables to a 2-quart glass jar or nonreactive bowl. Pour in the cooking liquid, adding water if necessary to completely cover the vegetables. Cover and refrigerate overnight before serving. (The pickled vegetables will keep up to 2 months in the refrigerator.)

3 cups water

1½ cups red wine vinegar

1 medium onion, sliced

2 garlic cloves, crushed

1 tablespoon kosher salt (or 1¾ teaspoons noniodized table salt)

2 teaspoons dried tarragon

2 teaspoons granulated sugar

½ teaspoon black peppercorns

2 cups cauliflower florets (about ½ head)

3 medium carrots, cut diagonally into ¼-inch-thick slices

2 large celery ribs, cut diagonally into ½-inch-thick slices

Ricardo's Chile con Queso

When I serve a Mexican meal, I put out a mini-crockpot with this cheesy dip, surrounded by tortilla chips, and it disappears in no time.

Makes about 2 cups

1. Preheat a 1-quart slow cooker while you prepare the chorizo mixture.

2. In a large skillet over medium heat, cook the chorizo, onion, and chile pepper, stirring often, until the chorizo is beginning to brown, about 6 minutes. Drain off the excess fat.

3. Add the tomatoes and garlic and cook, stirring often, until the tomatoes have given off their liquid and it has evaporated, about 5 minutes. Transfer the chorizo mixture to the slow cooker.

4. Add the Monterey Jack cheese in batches, stirring until each addition is partially melted before adding another. Cover and slow-cook, stirring often, until the cheese is completely melted, about 1 hour.

5. Uncover and serve with tortilla chips for dipping. The slow cooker will keep the dip at proper serving temperature for 3 hours.

2 2-ounce chorizo sausages or other spicy smoked sausage, cut into 1/4-inch cubes

1 medium onion, chopped

1 fresh hot green chile pepper (such as jalapeño), seeded and minced, or 2 tablespoons chopped canned chiles

1 15-ounce can peeled Italian tomatoes, drained and chopped

2 garlic cloves, minced

2 cups shredded Monterey Jack cheese (about 8 ounces)

Tortilla chips

Italian Fonduto

This Italian version of Swiss fondue comes from the northern part of the country, just over the border from Switzerland, in fact. However, it uses milk as its base, not wine. *Fonduto* is best made with Italian Val d'Aosta Fontina cheese, not Swedish Fontina. In season, white truffles are shaved over the top, making it a luxurious cheese dip indeed.

Makes 4 to 6 servings

1 cup evaporated milk

4 teaspoons all-purpose flour

4 cups cubed Fontina cheese, preferably Italian (about 1 pound)

1 garlic clove, peeled

2 egg yolks

⅛ teaspoon freshly ground white pepper

Breadsticks and fresh vegetable crudités

1. In a deep, medium saucepan, slowly whisk the milk into the flour until smooth. Bring to a simmer over low heat, whisking often. Gradually add the cheese, stirring to melt each addition before adding another.

2. Rub the inside of a 1-quart slow cooker with the garlic clove, and discard the garlic. Whisk the egg yolks and pepper together in the slow cooker. Gradually beat in the cheese mixture.

3. The slow cooker will keep the *fonduto* at proper serving temperature for about 2 hours. Serve with breadsticks and crudités for dipping.

Basil Fonduto: *Stir ¼ cup Pistou (page 36) into the* fonduto *just before serving.*

Bagna Cauda

This "hot bath" of olive oil, butter, anchovies, and garlic is a heady Italian dip. Finger-shaped pieces of crusty Italian bread can be dipped in addition to the customary raw vegetables.

Makes 6 to 8 servings

1. In a 1-quart slow cooker, combine the oil, butter, anchovies, and garlic. Cover and slow-cook until the butter has melted, about 1 hour.

2. Uncover and serve with crudités. The slow cooker will keep the dip at the proper serving temperature for about 4 hours. (Remove the garlic clove if it begins to brown.)

¾ cup extra-virgin olive oil

8 tablespoons (1 stick) unsalted butter

6 anchovy fillets, mashed to a paste

1 garlic clove, crushed

Fresh vegetable crudités, such as carrots, celery, cauliflower, and broccoli

Lamb and Pine-Nut–Stuffed Grape Leaves

Plump stuffed grape leaves are an excellent appetizer, served with a bowl of yogurt for dipping. I have collected recipes from Greek, Israeli, and Syrian friends, who all warn about the grape leaves scorching in the bottom of the pot on the stove. I have solved this burning issue by cooking them in the slow cooker.

Makes about 4 dozen

1. In a large saucepan of boiling water, cook the grape leaves for 1 minute. Drain, rinse well under cold running water, and drain again. Pick through the grape leaves and choose about 48 of the largest ones for stuffing; reserve the smaller leaves for separating the grape leaf layers.

2. Bring a medium saucepan of lightly salted boiling water to a boil over medium heat. Add the rice and cook just until tender, about 8 minutes. Drain, rinse well under cold running water, and drain again.

3. In a large skillet over medium-high heat, cook the ground lamb, onion, pine nuts, and garlic, stirring often to break up lumps, until the meat loses its pink color, about 6 minutes. Drain off the excess fat. Stir in the drained rice, mint, currants, 1 tablespoon of the lemon juice, the salt, and pepper.

4. Place a grape leaf, veined side up, on a work surface. Place about 1½ tablespoons of the ground lamb filling in the center. Fold

1 16-ounce jar grape leaves, drained

¾ cup converted long-grain rice

1 pound lean ground lamb or ground sirloin

1 medium onion, finely chopped

¼ cup pine nuts

1 garlic clove, minced

¼ cup chopped fresh mint or 1 tablespoon dried mint

¼ cup currants or raisins

¼ cup lemon juice, divided

1 teaspoon salt

¼ teaspoon freshly ground black pepper

1 teaspoon olive oil

1 cup water

over the sides, then roll up the grape leaf to form a cylinder. Repeat the procedure with the remaining leaves and filling.

5. Brush the inside of a 3½-quart slow cooker crockery insert with the olive oil. Arrange the stuffed grape leaves in closely packed layers, separating each layer with some of the reserved small leaves. Cover the stuffed leaves with the remaining small leaves. In a measuring cup, combine the remaining 3 tablespoons lemon juice with the water, and pour over the grape leaves. Cover the grape leaves with a circle of waxed or parchment paper.

6. Cover and slow-cook until the grape leaves are cooked through, about 4 hours on low (200°F). Let cool to room temperature before serving.

Veal, Pork, and Spinach Pâté

Makes 6 to 8 servings

1. In a small skillet, heat the oil over low heat. Add the shallots and garlic and cook, stirring often, until softened, about 2 minutes. Transfer to a large bowl.

2. Add the ground veal, ground pork, spinach, bread crumbs, heavy cream, vermouth, cognac, egg, salt, thyme, allspice, and pepper and mix well. Line a 6-cup soufflé dish with the bacon strips, letting the ends hang over the sides. Pack the meat mixture into the dish and top with the bay leaf. Fold the bacon ends over to cover the meat mixture. Cover the dish with foil.

3. Place an inverted custard cup in a 5-quart slow cooker. Pour in 2 cups hot water. Place the soufflé dish in the slow cooker and cook until a meat thermometer inserted in the center of the pâté (right through the foil) reads 165°F, about 3 hours on high (300°F) or 6 to 7 hours on low (200°F). Let the terrine stand in the slow cooker until cool enough to handle.

4. Place the dish, still covered with foil, on a large plate. Place a smaller plate on top of the pâté, one that will fit into the dish. Weigh the plate down with something heavy and refrigerate overnight.

5. Remove the foil and run a sharp knife around the inside of the soufflé dish. Invert the pâté onto a plate. Scrape off and discard the congealed juices from the pâté. To serve, cut the pâté into thin wedges.

1 tablespoon olive oil

4 medium shallots, minced

1 garlic clove, minced

1 pound ground veal

1 pound ground pork

1 10-ounce package chopped spinach, defrosted and squeezed to remove excess moisture

½ cup fresh bread crumbs

¼ cup heavy cream

2 tablespoons dry vermouth

2 tablespoons Cognac or brandy

1 large egg, beaten

2 teaspoons salt

1 teaspoon dried thyme

¼ teaspoon ground allspice

¼ teaspoon freshly ground black pepper

4 slices bacon

1 bay leaf

Soups and Chilis

The leisurely simmering of the slow cooker makes it ideal for preparing a big pot of soup or chili. Served with a fresh salad and some crusty bread, these dishes can be the centerpiece of a simple, tasty meal.

Most of the soups here are fork-and-knife affairs, something to really dig your teeth into. While some of them could be served as first courses at more formal dinners, I think they work best standing on their own as the centerpiece of a casual meal for friends and family. Soup is a versatile dish, indeed. For example, the Jamaican Oxtail Soup is full of complex flavors, with Caribbean spices and loads of beef and vegetables. While intriguingly spiced, the Curried Chicken and Apple Soup is somewhat less hearty. The light eaters in your family will go for the Mediterranean Vegetable Soup with Pistou. When I first moved to New York, I used to make lots of Beefy Borscht in my slow cooker to feed legions of unemployed actor friends. Even when it's steaming hot in the kitchen, cool soup prepared in the slow cooker can be the bill of fare. Enjoy vegetarian minestrone as they do in Italy at outdoor cafés, served at room temperature. (If you are adapting a favorite recipe to the slow cooker, take into consideration your appliance's size. The most popular size is 3½ quarts, about half the size of a standard soup pot.)

Chili, that all-American "bowl of red," is often a matter of some controversy. Some aficionados insist that true chili should not include tomatoes. Others argue that it should be made with chopped, not ground, meat. In certain areas of the Southwest, you're asking for a showdown if your chili has beans in it. Everyone agrees on one thing: Chili *must* be cooked slowly. The slow cooker makes the best chili this side of the Rio Grande, as the spices thoroughly infuse the meat while it simmers to tenderness. There's something here for every chili lover, from No-Beans, No-Tomatoes, No-Foolin' Chili to Vegetable-Garbanzo Chili to Turkey and Hominy Chili. While I prefer my chili with just a dollop of sour cream or yogurt, offer all kinds of toppings—grated Cheddar cheese, chopped onions, scallions, or pickled chile peppers, or sliced black olives.

Vegetarian Stock

The secret to a good vegetable stock is to include potato skins and use plenty of garlic. While stock is meant to be used as an ingredient in other dishes, you may find yourself sipping this one on its own.

Makes about 1½ quarts

1. Combine all of the ingredients in a 3½-quart slow cooker. Cover and slow-cook until the vegetables are very tender, 7 to 8 hours on low (200°F) or 3 to 3½ hours on high (300°F).

2. Strain the vegetables through a sieve set over a large bowl. Discard the vegetables and let the broth cool completely. (The broth can be refrigerated covered, for up to 4 days, or frozen up to 1 month.)

2 medium onions, chopped

2 medium carrots, chopped

2 medium celery ribs, with leaves, chopped

2 medium baking potatoes (such as Idaho), scrubbed, unpeeled and cut into 1-inch-thick rounds

1 head garlic, unpeeled, cut in half horizontally

4 parsley sprigs

½ teaspoon salt

⅛ teaspoon black peppercorns

1½ quarts water

Double-Strength Chicken or Beef Stock

One of the building blocks of good cooking is a full-flavored stock. For years, I have used the slow cooker to make rich, clear stocks that I can use in both conventional and slow-cooked cuisine. Stock becomes cloudy if it boils, because the fast cooking suspends the fats and bone gelatin in the liquid. When this happens, even tedious clarification won't get the stock perfectly clear. Since slow cookers don't boil on the low setting, and they allow the meat and vegetables to slowly release every drop of flavor, they make flawless stock. I never salt homemade stock, because if it reduces during cooking, the salt flavor will intensify.

Makes about 1½ quarts

4 pounds chicken necks or backs, skin removed, or 4 pounds meaty beef bones

1 medium onion, unpeeled, halved

2 medium carrots, coarsely chopped

2 medium celery ribs, coarsely chopped

4 parsley sprigs

1 teaspoon dried thyme

1 bay leaf

¼ teaspoon black peppercorns

2 quarts water

1. Position a broiler rack 6 inches from the source of heat and preheat the broiler. Broil the chicken or the beef bones, turning often, until well browned, 15 to 20 minutes. Transfer to a 3½-quart slow cooker.

2. Add the onion (the peel adds color to the stock), carrots, celery, parsley, thyme, bay leaf, and peppercorns. Pour in the water. Cover and slow-cook until the meat and vegetables are very tender, 10 to 12 hours on low (200°F). (Do not cook on high for a shorter period of time or the stock will boil and become cloudy.)

3. Ladle the stock through a strainer set over a large bowl. Discard the meat and vegetables. Let the stock cool to room temperature, then cover and refrigerate. When cold, scrape the congealed fat from the surface of the stock. (The stock can be refrigerated, covered, for up to 2 days or it can be frozen for up to 3 months.)

Glace de Viande: *Every fine French chef has a supply of* glace de viande *(an unsalted stock that has been reduced down to a thick glaze) to spoon into dishes that need a boost of concentrated meat flavor. My friend Bev Mortensen, a cooking school administrator for King's Markets in New Jersey, makes her* glace de viande *in the slow cooker. When made on top of the stove,* glace de viande *needs close attention, or it will scorch on the bottom of the saucepan. The slow cooker's even heating solves that problem. In a medium saucepan, bring 6 cups of Double-Strength Beef Stock to a boil over high heat. Transfer to a preheated 3½-quart slow cooker and cook until the stock has thickened and reduced to about 1½ cups, about 8 hours on high (300°F).*

Beefy Borscht

There are as many recipes for borscht as there are cooks in Eastern Europe. And every cook has a list of ingredients that should never go into the borscht pot. Tomatoes are on a lot of those lists, but in fact they complement the beets in both flavor and color. Indulge in a big dollop of cool sour cream to top the steaming borscht.

Makes 4 to 6 servings

1. In a large skillet, heat the oil over medium-high heat. Add the beef and cook, turning often, until browned on all sides. Transfer the beef to a plate and season with the salt and pepper.

2. Add more oil to the skillet, if necessary, and heat. Add the onion, carrots, celery, and bell pepper. Reduce the heat to medium, and cook, stirring often, until the onions are softened, about 5 minutes. Add the garlic and cook, stirring often, for 1 minute. Add the water and stir to scrape up the browned bits on the bottom of the skillet. Transfer to a 3½-quart slow cooker and add the beets and potatoes. Then add the beef, beef broth, tomatoes with their

2 tablespoons vegetable oil, plus more if needed

1 pound boneless beef bottom round, cut into 1-inch pieces

1 teaspoon salt

½ teaspoon freshly ground black pepper

1 large onion, chopped

2 medium carrots, cut into ½-inch-thick rounds

2 medium celery ribs, cut into ½-inch-thick slices

1 medium green bell pepper, seeded and cut into ½-inch cubes

2 garlic cloves, minced

2 cups water

4 medium beets, peeled and cut into ½-inch cubes (about 1 pound)

2 medium boiling potatoes, scrubbed, unpeeled, and cut into ½-inch cubes

2⅔ cups double-strength beef broth, canned or homemade

juice, the tomato paste, vinegar, brown sugar, thyme, and caraway seeds. Break up the tomatoes with the side of a spoon, then cover and slow-cook until the meat is tender, 6 to 7 hours on low (200°F).

3. Spoon the soup into individual bowls, and top each serving with a dollop of sour cream.

1 15-ounce can peeled Italian tomatoes, undrained, coarsely chopped

1/4 cup tomato paste

2 tablespoons red wine vinegar

1 tablespoon light brown sugar

2 teaspoons dried thyme

1 teaspoon caraway seeds

Sour cream, for garnish

Country-Style Onion and Cheese Soup

In restaurants, bowls of onion soup are capped with toasted French bread, sprinkled with Gruyère cheese and broiled to melt the cheese. At home, this process is awkward, so follow the advice of my sensible French friend: Layer the bread and cheese in a soup tureen, and pour the soup over.

Makes 6 to 8 servings

1.   In a large skillet, melt the butter over medium heat. Add the red and yellow onions. Cover the skillet and cook, stirring occasionally, until the onions are softened, about 15 minutes. Stir in the sugar, salt, and pepper. Continue cooking, uncovered, stirring occasionally, until the onions are golden brown, 20 to 30 minutes. Transfer the onions to a 3½-quart slow cooker.

2.   Add the wine to the skillet and bring to a boil over medium-high heat, scraping up the browned bits on the bottom of the skillet with a wooden spoon. Add the wine, beef broth, water, and thyme to the slow cooker and stir well. Cover and slow-cook for 5 to 6 hours on low (200°F).

3.   Meanwhile, preheat the oven to 400°F. Place the bread slices on two baking sheets and brush with the olive oil. Bake until the bread slices are toasted, 10 to 15 minutes.

4.   Place half the bread slices in a soup tureen and sprinkle with half of the cheese; then repeat the layering. Pour the hot soup into the tureen. Cover and let stand for 5 minutes before serving.

4 tablespoons unsalted butter

2 large red onions, thinly sliced

2 large yellow onions, thinly sliced

1 teaspoon sugar

½ teaspoon salt

¼ teaspoon freshly ground black pepper

½ cup dry white wine or dry vermouth

2⅔ cups double-strength beef broth, canned or homemade

2 cups water

½ teaspoon dried thyme

8 large slices French or Italian bread

¼ cup olive oil

2 cups grated Gruyère or Swiss cheese (about 8 ounces)

Mediterranean Vegetable Soup with Pistou

The French call it *pistou,* the Italians call it *pesto.* No matter what the terminology, Americans have taken the basil and cheese purée to their hearts. Here's a soup that is just as good served at room temperature on a warm afternoon as it is piping hot on a chilly night.

Makes 4 to 6 servings

1. In a large skillet, heat the oil over medium heat. Add the onion, leek, carrots, zucchini, green beans, and cook, stirring often, until the onions are softened, about 6 minutes. Add the garlic and cook, stirring often, for 1 minute. Transfer to a 3½-quart slow cooker.

2. Stir in the chicken broth, water, tomatoes with their juice, the parsley, salt, and pepper. Cover and slow-cook until the vegetables are tender, 6 to 7 hours on low (200°F).

3. Increase the heat to high (300°F). Stir in the pasta and cook until tender, about 30 minutes.

4. Spoon the soup into individual bowls. Pass bowls of Pistou and grated cheese and let guests add them to taste.

3 tablespoons olive oil

1 medium onion, chopped

1 large leek, chopped (or 1 additional onion)

2 medium carrots, cut into ½-inch-thick rounds

2 medium zucchini, peeled and cut into 1-inch-thick rounds

¼ pound green beans, cut into 1-inch pieces

2 garlic cloves, minced

2⅔ cups double-strength chicken broth, canned or homemade

2 cups water

1 15-ounce can peeled Italian tomatoes, undrained, coarsely chopped

2 tablespoons chopped fresh parsley

1 teaspoon salt

¼ teaspoon freshly ground black pepper

½ cup small tubular pasta

Pistou (recipe follows)

Freshly grated imported Parmesan cheese

Pistou

Don't limit your pistou use to tossing with pasta or spooning into soup. Try it as a condiment for grilled chicken or swordfish, or as a topping for baked potatoes.

Makes ²/₃ cup

In a blender, combine the basil, Parmesan cheese, nuts, garlic, salt, and pepper. With the machine running, gradually pour in the oil and process to a smooth paste. (The pistou can be covered and refrigerated for up to 1 day. For storage up to 2 weeks, pour a thin layer of olive oil over the surface of the pistou and refrigerate.)

2 cups loosely packed fresh basil leaves, well rinsed

¼ cup freshly grated imported Parmesan cheese

¼ cup pine nuts or walnuts

2 garlic cloves, crushed

¼ teaspoon salt

⅛ teaspoon freshly ground black pepper

⅓ cup plus 1 tablespoon olive oil

Summer Garden Vegetarian Minestrone

During the dog days of summer, I often serve this soup at room temperature for supper. Packed full of vegetables, it is as light and refreshing as a salad. If you don't have vegetable stock on hand, you can substitute vegetable bouillon cubes and water.

Makes 4 to 6 servings

1. In a large skillet, heat the oil over medium heat. Add the onion, carrots, celery, bell pepper, and zucchini and cook, stirring often, until the onion is softened, about 6 minutes. Add the garlic and cook, stirring often, for 1 minute. Transfer to a 3½-quart slow cooker.

2. Add the Vegetarian Stock, tomatoes with their purée, the marjoram, salt, and pepper, breaking up the tomatoes with the side of a spoon. Cover and slow-cook until the vegetables are tender, 6 to 7 hours on low (200°F).

3. Meanwhile, in a large saucepan of boiling salted water, cook the cabbage and rice together until the rice is tender, about 15 minutes. Drain well.

4. Stir the cabbage and rice into the soup and slow-cook for an additional 15 minutes. Stir in the chopped basil. Serve the soup hot, warm, or at room temperature.

When cooking with fresh herbs, stir them into soups and sauces towards the end of the cooking time. If added too soon, their delicate oils will evaporate, and their flavor will be lost.

2 tablespoons olive oil

1 medium onion, chopped

2 medium carrots, cut into ½-inch rounds

2 medium celery ribs, cut into ½-inch pieces

1 red bell pepper, seeded and cut into ½-inch cubes

1 medium zucchini, scrubbed and cut into ½-inch rounds

2 garlic cloves, minced

5 cups Vegetarian Stock (page 29)

1 28-ounce can peeled Italian tomatoes in thick tomato purée

2 teaspoons dried marjoram

1 teaspoon salt

¼ teaspoon freshly ground black pepper

2 cups shredded cabbage (about ½ small head)

½ cup converted long-grain rice

3 tablespoons chopped fresh basil or parsley

Beef Goulash Pot

Goulash, or *guylas,* can be either a thin but tasty soup, or a gutsy, gravied stew. I've decided to meet somewhere in the middle. No matter what, real Hungarian paprika is a *must.* It comes in two varieties, sweet and hot. The sweet variety is the most versatile, but aficionados of spicy flavors will love the hotter version. Once you've tasted real paprika, you'll never return to the pallid stuff that is usually found on most spice racks.

1. In a large skillet, heat the oil over medium-high heat. Add the beef in batches, without crowding, and cook, turning often, until browned on all sides. Transfer to a plate and season with the salt and pepper.

2. Add more oil to the skillet, if necessary, and heat. Add the onion and bell pepper. Reduce the heat to medium and cook, stirring often, until softened, about 5 minutes. Add the flour, garlic, paprika, and caraway seeds and stir for 1 minute.

3. Place the potatoes in the bottom of a 3½-quart slow cooker. Add the beef and the vegetable mixture. Pour in the beef broth, water, and tomato purée. Cover and slow-cook until the beef is tender, 6 to 7 hours on low (200°F).

4. Serve the soup in individual bowls, topping each serving with a dollop of sour cream.

2 tablespoons vegetable oil, plus more if needed

1 pound boneless beef bottom round, cut into 1-inch cubes

1 teaspoon salt

¼ teaspoon freshly ground black pepper

1 large onion, chopped

1 medium green bell pepper, seeded and sliced

¼ cup all-purpose flour

2 garlic cloves, minced

3 tablespoons sweet Hungarian paprika

1 teaspoon caraway seeds

2 medium boiling potatoes, scrubbed, unpeeled, and cut into ½-inch rounds

2⅔ cups double-strength beef broth, canned or homemade

1½ cups water

1 cup tomato purée

Sour cream, for garnish

Curried Chicken and Apple Soup

Also known as mulligatawny, this soup gets an added boost of flavor from freshly squeezed apple cider. Sautéing the curry powder briefly helps to "open up" its flavor.

Makes 4 to 6 servings

1. In a large skillet, heat the oil over medium-high heat. Add the chicken thighs, skin side down, and cook until browned, about 3 minutes. (Do not turn the chicken.) Transfer the chicken to a 3½-quart slow cooker and season with the salt and pepper.

2. Pour off all but 2 tablespoons fat from the skillet. Add the onion and celery to the skillet, adding more oil if necessary, and reduce the heat to medium. Cook, stirring often, until the onion is softened, about 5 minutes. Add the flour, curry powder, and garlic and stir for 30 seconds. Gradually stir in the chicken broth and bring to a simmer. Transfer to the slow cooker.

3. Stir the water and apple cider into the slow cooker, cover, and slow-cook until the chicken is tender, 5 to 6 hours on low (200°F).

4. Remove the chicken thighs from the soup, discard the skin, and remove the meat from the bones. Coarsely chop the meat and return to the slow cooker. Stir in the heavy cream, and cook for 5 minutes.

5. Place a large spoonful of cooked rice in each soup bowl. Spoon the soup into the bowls, and sprinkle each serving with chopped apple.

1 tablespoon vegetable oil, plus more if needed

6 chicken thighs (about 2 pounds)

¾ teaspoon salt

¼ teaspoon freshly ground black pepper

1 large onion, chopped

2 medium celery ribs, chopped

3 tablespoons all-purpose flour

2 tablespoons curry powder, preferably Madras

2 garlic cloves, minced

2⅔ cups double-strength chicken broth, canned or homemade

3½ cups water

½ cup freshly squeezed apple cider

½ cup heavy cream

3 cups hot cooked rice

1 medium Granny Smith apple, peeled, cored, and finely chopped, for garnish

Chinese Chicken Hot Pot

Other vegetables, such as zucchini, mushrooms, and sweet red peppers, can be added as desired to this colorful main-course soup. To round out your Oriental meal, serve this with Chinese Cabbage and Peanut Slaw (page 227).

Makes 4 to 6 servings

1. In a 3½-quart slow cooker, combine the water, chicken broth, onion, carrots, celery, water chestnuts, soy sauce, ginger, garlic, and crushed red pepper. Cover and slow-cook until the vegetables are tender, 6 to 7 hours on low (200°F).

2. Turn the heat to high (300°F) and add the chicken, tofu, snow peas, and scallions. Cover and slow-cook until the chicken is firm, about 15 minutes. Serve immediately.

3 cups water

2⅔ cups double-strength chicken broth, canned or homemade

1 medium onion, thinly sliced

2 medium carrots, cut diagonally into ½-inch-thick pieces

2 medium celery ribs, cut diagonally into ½-inch-thick pieces

1 8-ounce can water chestnuts, drained and sliced

2 teaspoons soy sauce

2 ¼-inch-thick slices ginger

2 garlic cloves, crushed

¼ teaspoon crushed hot red pepper

1 pound boneless skinless chicken cutlets, trimmed and cut diagonally into ½-inch-thick slices

8 ounces firm tofu, cut into 1-inch cubes

2 ounces snow peas, trimmed

2 medium scallions, chopped

Guacamole Salsa

The two most popular Mexican condiments, guacamole and salsa, join forces here to make an exuberant relish that can be used to add spice to a variety of dishes. While it adds zip to slow-cooked bean dishes, I also use it to accompany plain grilled chicken breasts or fish. Use the pebble-skinned Haas avocados, and avoid the huge but tasteless Florida varieties.

Makes about 2 cups

Here's an efficient way to peel avocados: Using a sharp knife, cut all the way around the avocado from top to bottom (the blade will touch the large pit in the center). Twist the two halves gently in different directions and pull apart to reveal the pit, which will remain in one of the halves. Using a large serving spoon, dig out and discard the pit, then scoop the avocado flesh out of the skin.

In a medium bowl, combine all the ingredients. Cover and refrigerate for 1 hour before serving. (The salsa can be prepared up to 8 hours before serving, covered, and refrigerated—but remember that freshness is part of this condiment's appeal.)

6 ripe plum tomatoes (about 1 pound), seeded and chopped

2 ripe Haas avocados, peeled, pitted, and chopped

3 tablespoons minced onion

2 tablespoons minced fresh cilantro (optional)

1 garlic clove, minced

1 fresh hot green chile pepper (such as jalapeño), seeded and minced

4 teaspoons lime or lemon juice

3/4 teaspoon salt

Chicken, Tomato, and Tortilla Soup

This is one of my favorite soups—a spicy tomato broth studded with tender chunks of chicken and topped with crisp tortilla strips.

Makes 4 to 6 servings

1. In a large skillet over medium-high heat, cook the chicken thighs, skin side down, until the skin is golden brown, about 3 minutes. (Do not turn the chicken.) Transfer the chicken to a 3½-quart slow cooker. Discard all of the fat in the skillet.

2. In a food processor or blender, purée the tomatoes with their juice, the onion, chile pepper, and garlic. Add to the skillet and cook over medium heat, stirring often, until slightly thickened, about 3 minutes. Add the tomato mixture, water, chicken broth, cumin, salt, pepper, and bay leaf to the slow cooker and stir well.

3. Cover and slow-cook until the chicken thighs are tender, 5 to 6 hours on low (200°F).

4. Remove the chicken thighs and cool slightly. When the chicken is cool enough to handle, discard the skin and remove the meat from the bones. Coarsely chop the chicken meat and return to the slow cooker. Stir in the corn and chopped cilantro.

5. Meanwhile, preheat the oven to 400°F. Lightly brush both sides of the tortillas with the oil. Using a sharp knife, cut the tortillas into strips about 2 inches long and ½ inch wide. Spread the tortilla strips on a baking sheet. Bake, stirring occasionally, until crisp and golden brown, 5 to 8 minutes.

6 chicken thighs (about 2 pounds)

1 15-ounce can peeled Italian tomatoes

1 medium onion, chopped

1 fresh hot green chile pepper (such as jalapeño), seeded and chopped

1 garlic clove, crushed

3 cups water

2⅔ cups double-strength chicken broth, canned or homemade

1 teaspoon ground cumin

1 teaspoon salt

¼ teaspoon freshly ground black pepper

1 bay leaf

1 10-ounce package frozen corn, defrosted

2 tablespoons chopped fresh cilantro

4 corn tortillas

1 tablespoon vegetable oil

Guacamole Salsa, optional (recipe precedes)

Lime wedges, for garnish

Freshly grated Romano cheese, for garnish

6.   Remove the bay leaf from the soup. Serve the soup in individual bowls, topping each serving with crisp tortilla strips and a dollop of Guacamole Salsa, if desired. Let each guest squeeze on lime juice to taste, and pass a bowl of grated cheese for sprinkling.

Lamb, Split Pea, and Dill Soup

The addition of lamb to split pea soup makes a nice change from the usual ham, and dill adds a Scandinavian accent. To be authentically Scandinavian, use yellow split peas.

Makes 4 to 6 servings

1. In a large bowl, combine the split peas and water; let stand overnight.

2. Transfer the peas and water to a saucepan, bring to a boil over high heat, and cook for 5 minutes. Transfer to a 3½-quart slow cooker.

3. In a large skillet, heat the oil over medium-high heat. Cook the lamb in batches, without crowding, turning often, until browned on all sides. Add the lamb to the slow cooker and season with the salt and pepper.

4. Add more oil to the skillet, if necessary, and heat. Add the onion, carrots, and celery and reduce the heat to medium. Cook, stirring often, until the onion is softened, about 5 minutes. Transfer to the slow cooker. Pour in the chicken broth. Cover and slow-cook until the peas are tender, 7 to 8 hours on low (200°F).

5. Stir the dill into the soup and serve immediately.

1 pound dried yellow or green split peas, rinsed, drained, and picked over

4 cups water

2 tablespoons vegetable oil, plus more if needed

1½ pounds boneless lamb shoulder, cut into 2-inch cubes

1 teaspoon salt

¼ teaspoon freshly ground black pepper

1 large onion, chopped

2 medium carrots, cut into ½-inch rounds

2 medium celery, cut into ½-inch slices

2⅔ cups double-strength chicken broth, canned or homemade

2 tablespoons chopped fresh dill

Black Bean and Smoked Turkey Soup

While I often serve this dark-hued, smokey-flavored soup unadorned, I can't resist the temptation to add accents of color and flavor with dollops of salsa and sour cream. Serve big bowls of the soup with crisp tortilla chips and green salad.

Makes 6 to 8 servings

1. In a large pot, combine the beans and enough cold water to cover by 2 inches. Bring to a boil over high heat, then boil for 2 minutes. Remove from the heat, cover the pot, and let stand for 1 hour; drain well. (The beans can also be presoaked overnight in a large bowl with enough water to cover by 2 inches, then drained.)

2. In a 3½-quart slow cooker, combine the drained beans with the turkey wing pieces, onion, carrots, and celery. Pour in the chicken broth and water.

3. Cover and slow-cook until the beans and vegetables are very tender, 8 to 10 hours on low (200°F). Stir in the sherry, salt, and pepper.

4. Using kitchen tongs, transfer the turkey wing pieces to a plate and let cool slightly. Using a slotted spoon, transfer the solids in the soup to a food processor. Pulse until coarsely puréed, then stir into the cooking liquid. Remove the meat from the wings and coarsely chop, discarding the skin and bones. Stir the turkey meat into the soup.

5. Serve the soup in individual bowls and garnish each portion with dollops of Guacamole Salsa and sour cream.

1 pound dried black beans, rinsed, drained, and picked over

1 pound smoked turkey wings, chopped into 2-inch pieces

1 large onion, chopped

3 medium carrots, chopped

3 medium celery ribs, chopped

2⅔ cups double-strength chicken broth, canned or homemade

3 cups water

⅓ cup dry sherry or Madeira

½ teaspoon salt

¼ teaspoon freshly ground black pepper

Guacamole Salsa (page 41), for garnish

Sour cream, for garnish

Turkey, Escarole, and White Bean Soup

The last time I was in Italy, I did plenty of cooking in the kitchen of my friends Fabio and Diane. Every morning we would stroll through their village near Lake Como to choose our groceries, and this soup was created for a rainy afternoon meal-in-a-pot. Their butcher always had lots of turkey parts, as Italians regularly braise drumsticks in soups and stews or use boneless turkey breast to stand in for the pricier veal scallopine. Although escarole resembles a head of lettuce, it has a bitter quality that must be tamed by blanching before adding it to soup. That being done, it makes a lovely counterpoint to the neutrally flavored beans.

Makes 6 to 8 servings

1. In a medium saucepan, combine the beans and enough cold water to cover by 2 inches. Bring to a boil over high heat, then boil for 2 minutes. Remove from the heat, cover the pan, and let stand for 1 hour; drain well. (The beans can also be presoaked overnight in a medium bowl with enough water to cover by 2 inches, then drained.)

2. Transfer the beans to a 3½-quart slow cooker. Stir in the onion, carrot, celery, garlic, parsley, and pepper.

3. In a large skillet, heat the oil over medium-high heat. Add the drumsticks and cook, turning occasionally, until browned on all

4 ounces dried cannellini (white kidney beans), rinsed, drained, and picked over

1 medium onion, chopped

1 medium carrot, chopped

1 medium celery rib, chopped

2 garlic cloves, minced

2 tablespoons chopped fresh parsley

¼ teaspoon freshly ground black pepper

1 tablespoon olive oil

3 turkey drumsticks (about 12 ounces each)

4¼ cups water

1⅔ cups double-strength chicken broth, canned or homemade

1 teaspoon salt

1 head escarole (about 10 ounces), cut crosswise into 1-inch-wide strips and well rinsed

Freshly grated imported Parmesan cheese

sides, about 8 minutes. Transfer the drumsticks, meaty side down, to the slow cooker. Pour in the water and broth.

4. Cover and slow-cook until the drumsticks and beans are tender, 6 to 7 hours on low (200°F). Remove the drumsticks and cool slightly. When the drumsticks are cool enough to handle, discard the skin. Remove the meat from the bones and discard the hard tendons. Coarsely chop the turkey meat and return to the slow cooker. Stir in the salt.

5. Meanwhile, bring a large saucepan of lightly salted water to a boil over medium-high heat. Add the escarole and cook until tender, about 5 minutes. Drain well.

6. Stir the escarole into the soup. Serve the soup with a bowl of grated cheese on the side for sprinkling.

Portuguese Kale and Sausage Soup

Caldo verde, while practically the national dish of Portugal, can be found in the most unlikely places. I have seen it served in Hawaii, on Cape Cod, and in Newark, New Jersey, although I must admit that all of these locations have large Portuguese communities. If you can't locate linguiça, that exceptional garlic-and-spice smoked sausage, chorizo, or even kielbasa will suffice.

Makes 4 to 6 servings

1. In a large skillet, heat 2 tablespoons of the oil over medium-high heat. Add the onion and cook, stirring often, until softened, about 5 minutes. Add the garlic and cook, stirring often, for 1 minute. Transfer to a 3½-quart slow cooker.

2. Add the water, chicken broth, potatoes, salt, and red pepper to the slow cooker. Cover and slow-cook until the potatoes are tender, 6 to 7 hours on low (200°F).

3. Meanwhile, in a dry medium skillet over medium heat, cook the linguica, stirring often, until lightly browned, about 6 minutes. Using a slotted spoon, transfer the linguiça to paper towels to drain.

4. Increase the heat of the slow cooker to High (300°F). Roll up the kale leaves in bunches into cylinders and using a large sharp knife, cut crosswise to form very thin shreds. (You will have about 6 cups.) Stir the shredded kale into the soup. Add the sausage, cover, and cook until the kale is tender, about 30 minutes.

5. Serve the soup in individual bowls, drizzling each serving with some of the remaining 2 tablespoons olive oil.

¼ cup extra-virgin olive oil, divided

1 large onion, chopped

2 garlic cloves, minced

3 cups water

2⅔ cups double-strength chicken broth, canned or homemade

2 medium boiling potatoes (about 8 ounces), scrubbed, unpeeled, and cut into ½-inch rounds

½ teaspoon salt

¼ teaspoon crushed hot red pepper

8 ounces linguiça sausage, cut into ¼-inch-thick rounds

1 small bunch curly dark kale, stems removed and well rinsed

Jamaican Oxtail Soup

Unglamorous oxtails have a meat-to-bone ratio that results in a decidedly upscale soup broth. However, the oxtails will render quite a bit of fat, so be sure to degrease the soup thoroughly. If you have the time, cool the soup and refrigerate overnight so the fat solidifies and can be easily scraped off and discarded.

Makes 6 to 8 servings

1. Position a broiler rack 4 inches from the source of heat and preheat the broiler. Broil the oxtails, turning once, until browned, about 10 minutes. Transfer the oxtails to a plate and season with the salt and pepper.

2. In a 5-quart slow cooker, layer the potatoes, onion, carrots, celery, scallions, chile pepper, and garlic, in that order. Sprinkle with the thyme and allspice. Arrange the oxtails on top of the vegetables. Pour in the water and add the bay leaf.

3. Cover and slow-cook until the oxtails are very tender, 9 to 11 hours on low (200°F) or 4 to 5 hours on high (300°F). Skim the fat from the surface of the soup before serving.

Note: To make this soup in a 3½-quart slow cooker, use half the amount of the ingredients, with just enough water to barely cover the oxtails. Makes 4 servings.

4 pounds oxtails, well trimmed

1 teaspoon salt

¼ teaspoon freshly ground black pepper

2 medium red-skinned potatoes, scrubbed, unpeeled, and cut into ½-inch cubes

1 large onion, chopped

2 medium carrots, cut into ½-inch-thick rounds

2 medium celery ribs, cut into ½-inch-thick slices

4 scallions, chopped

1 fresh hot green chile pepper (such as jalapeño), seeded and minced

1 garlic clove, minced

1 teaspoon dried thyme

½ teaspoon ground allspice

5 cups water

1 bay leaf

Pozole

Pozole, a Mexican soup made with pork and hominy, is a chunky mixture of meat and vegetables barely held together with a little broth. Part of the fun of serving pozole is the collection of garnishes the guests are allowed to sprinkle on their servings.

Makes 6 to 8 servings

1. In a large skillet, heat the oil. Add the pork, in batches, and cook, turning occasionally, until lightly browned on all sides, about 5 minutes. Using a slotted spoon, transfer the pork to a 3½-quart slow cooker.

2. Add the zucchini, onion, and chile pepper to the skillet, adding additional oil if necessary. Cook, stirring often, until the onion is softened, about 5 minutes. Add the garlic and cook, stirring often, for 1 minute. Add the cooked vegetables, water, chicken broth, marjoram, oregano, salt, and pepper to the slow cooker and stir well.

3. Cover and slow-cook until the pork is tender, 5 to 6 hours on low (200°F). Stir in the hominy and cook until heated through, about 10 minutes.

4. Place the radishes, avocado, olives, limes, grated cheese, and chopped peppers in small bowls. Serve the soup in individual bowls, allowing each guest to add the garnishes to taste.

Note: You can also use 4½ pounds bone-in pork neck, which is normally cut into 2-inch pieces by the butcher.

2 tablespoons olive oil, plus more if needed

2 pounds boneless pork shoulder, cut into 1-inch cubes

2 medium zucchini, cut into ¾-inch-thick rounds

1 medium onion, chopped

1 fresh hot green chile pepper (such as jalapeño), seeded and minced

2 garlic cloves, minced

3 cups water

2⅔ cups double-strength chicken broth, canned or homemade

1½ teaspoons dried marjoram

1½ teaspoons dried oregano

½ teaspoon salt

¼ teaspoon freshly ground black pepper

1 16-ounce can hominy, drained and rinsed

Grated radishes, cubed avocado, sliced black olives, lime wedges, grated Monterey Jack cheese, chopped pickled jalapeño peppers, for garnish

Pink Bean and Pasta Soup with Ham

The menus of many Italian restaurants offer *pasta e fagioli,* which translates as "pasta and beans." It's served as a first course, but it's so filling, it's difficult to eat the main dish.

Makes 4 to 6 servings

1. In a large bowl, combine the beans and enough water to cover by 2 inches. Let stand overnight; drain well.

2. In a large skillet, heat the oil over medium-high heat. Add the ham, onion, and celery and cook, stirring often, until lightly browned, about 6 minutes. Add the garlic and cook, stirring often, for 1 minute. Add the chicken broth, stirring to scrape up the browned bits on the bottom of the skillet. Transfer to a 3½-quart slow cooker.

3. Add the drained beans, water, and tomato paste. Cover and slow-cook until the beans are almost tender, 7 to 8 hours on low (200°F).

4. Stir in the spaghetti, salt, and pepper. Increase the heat to high (300°F) and cook until the spaghetti is tender, about 30 minutes. Using a large spoon, crush enough of the beans against the sides of the slow cooker to reach the consistency you like. Serve immediately.

1 cup dried pink or cranberry beans, rinsed, drained, and picked over

2 tablespoons olive oil

½ pound smoked ham, chopped

1 medium onion, finely chopped

1 medium celery rib, finely chopped

2 garlic cloves, minced

2⅔ cups double-strength chicken broth, canned or homemade

3 cups water

¼ cup tomato paste

½ cup spaghetti broken into 1-inch pieces

¼ teaspoon salt

¼ teaspoon freshly ground black pepper

French Bean, Cabbage, and Pork Soup

In the southwest corner of France, this hearty soup, called *garbure*, contains goose *confit*, meat that is cooked and preserved in its own fat. I've adapted the dish to take advantage of readily available ingredients.

Makes 4 to 6 servings

1. In a large bowl, soak the beans overnight at room temperature in enough water to cover by 2 inches. Drain well.

2. In a large saucepan, combine the beans and enough water to cover by 2 inches and bring to a boil over medium heat. Reduce the heat to low and simmer until the beans are almost tender, about 30 minutes. Drain well.

3. In a 3½-quart slow cooker, combine the chicken broth, water, ham hock, drained beans, onions, carrots, potatoes, turnip, garlic, parsley, thyme, and pepper. Cover and slow cook until the beans are tender, 7 to 8 hours on low (200°F). Remove the ham hock from the soup. Discard the skin and remove the meat from the bone. Coarsely chop the meat and return to the soup.

4. Meanwhile, bring a large pot of water to a boil over high heat. Add the sausages and cook for 5 minutes. Add the cabbage and cook until the cabbage is tender and the sausages are cooked through, about 10 minutes longer. Drain well. Remove the sausages, cool slightly, and slice into ½-inch-thick pieces.

5. Stir the sausages, cabbage, and salt into the soup. Increase the heat to high (300°F), cover, and slow-cook for 15 minutes. Serve immediately.

1 cup dried cannellini (white kidney beans), rinsed, drained, and picked over

2⅔ cups double-strength chicken broth, canned or homemade

4 cups water

1 smoked ham hock (9 ounces)

2 medium onions, chopped

2 medium carrots, chopped

2 medium boiling potatoes (about 8 ounces), scrubbed but unpeeled and cut into ½-inch-thick cubes

1 medium turnip, scrubbed but unpeeled and cut into ½-inch cubes

4 garlic cloves, minced

2 tablespoons chopped fresh parsley

1 teaspoon dried thyme

¼ teaspoon freshly ground black pepper

1 pound fresh sweet Italian sausages, pricked with a fork

1 small head cabbage (about 1 pound), cored and shredded

½ teaspoon salt

Ground Beef Chili with Cornmeal Dumplings

Here's a mild chili that everyone in the family will love. If you want more spice, use a hot enchilada sauce, or add a little cayenne pepper to taste.

Makes 4 to 6 servings

1. In a large nonstick skillet over medium-high heat, cook the ground beef, onion, bell pepper, and garlic, stirring often to break up lumps, until the meat loses its pink color, about 5 minutes. Drain off excess fat, and transfer to a 3½-quart slow cooker. Stir in the enchilada sauce, tomato sauce, olives, chili powder, 1 teaspoon of the salt, the oregano, and cumin.

2. Cover and slow-cook for 7 to 8 hours. Skim the fat off the surface of the chili.

3. In a heavy-bottomed medium saucepan, bring the water and the remaining ½ teaspoon salt to a boil over medium heat. Gradually whisk in the cornmeal. Reduce the heat to low and cook, whisking constantly, until very thick, about 1 minute.

4. Drop the cornmeal mixture by tablespoons onto the chili. Increase the heat to high (300°F) and cook, covered, until the dumplings are cooked through, about 15 minutes. Sprinkle the dumplings with the cheese and serve immediately.

2 pounds lean ground beef or ground turkey

1 medium onion, chopped

1 medium green bell pepper, chopped

2 garlic cloves, minced

1 10-ounce can mild enchilada sauce

1 8-ounce can tomato sauce

1 6½-ounce can pitted ripe black olives, drained

2 tablespoons chili powder

1½ teaspoons salt, divided

1 teaspoon dried oregano

½ teaspoon ground cumin

2 cups water

1 cup yellow cornmeal, preferably stone-ground

4 ounces shredded Cheddar cheese (about 1 cup), divided

No-Beans, No-Tomatoes, No-Foolin' Chili

Many chili aficionados argue that true chili has no beans, no tomatoes, and no vegetables other than onions, peppers, and garlic. I say that chili is too good to have just one way to fix it, but when you taste this five-alarm bull's-eye, you will see the chili purists' point.

Makes 6 to 8 servings

1. In a large skillet, heat 2 tablespoons of the oil over medium-high heat. Add the beef in batches, without crowding, and cook, turning often and adding more oil as needed, until browned on all sides. Transfer to a 3½-quart slow cooker.

2. Add the remaining 2 tablespoons oil to the skillet and reduce the heat to medium. Add the onions, bell peppers, and chiles and cook, stirring often, until the onions are softened, about 7 minutes. Add the chili powder, garlic, oregano, cumin, and salt and stir for 30 seconds. Remove from the heat and add the beer, scraping up the browned bits on the bottom of the skillet. Pour the vegetable mixture into the slow cooker.

3. Cover and cook until the meat is tender, 6 to 7 hours on low (200°F).

¼ cup olive oil, divided, plus more if needed

3½ pounds boneless beef chuck or round, cut into 1-inch pieces and well trimmed

2 large onions, chopped

2 medium green bell peppers, seeded and chopped

2 fresh hot green chile peppers (such as jalapeño), seeded and minced

2 garlic cloves, minced

⅓ cup chili powder

1 tablespoon dried oregano

2 teaspoons ground cumin

1 teaspoon salt

1 cup beer

3 tablespoons yellow cornmeal, preferably stone-ground (optional)

Seafood Stews and Chowders

Fish is best quickly cooked, so it retains its moisture and texture. At first, it seemed that the slow cooker wouldn't produce acceptable seafood dishes. I was unhappy with the results I got trying to prepare whole fish fillets and steaks. (Not the least of the problem was how to get the cooked fish *out* of the cooker without it falling apart.) Finally, I solved the problem by devising a two-step procedure to create delicious seafood entrées.

All of the recipes offered here feature a savory broth with chunks of seafood and vegetables. First, a flavorful liquid base is slow-cooked and ten to fifteen minutes before serving I add bite-sized pieces of fish or seafood to the hot liquid for last-minute cooking.

With this method, it's possible to make Cioppino, a San Francisco seafood soup with a tomato and red wine base; New Orleans Seafood Etouffé and Snapper, Oyster, and Ham Gumbo; tomatoey Big Apple Scallop Chowder; and creamy Nor'eastern Shrimp Chowder. No matter what recipe you choose, take care not to overcook the seafood: Cook it just until firm.

Nor'eastern Shrimp Chowder

The original chowder was made by French Canadian fishermen in a huge cauldron called a *chaudière*. When the recipe traveled to Maine, the cooks there named the soup after the utensil it was cooked in, mispronouncing it "chowder." This slow-cooker recipe adds heavy cream at the end to give flavor and body, but you can use evaporated milk if you wish.

Makes 4 to 6 servings

4 strips bacon, cut into 1-inch pieces

1 medium onion, chopped

3 tablespoons all-purpose flour

4 medium boiling potatoes, scrubbed, unpeeled, and cut into 1/2-inch cubes

3 cups bottled clam juice

2 cups water

1/4 teaspoon dried thyme

1 bay leaf

1/4 teaspoon freshly ground white pepper

1 1/2 pounds medium shrimp, peeled and deveined

3/4 cup heavy cream

Salt to taste

Chopped fresh parsley, for garnish

1. In a medium skillet, cook the bacon over medium heat, turning often, until browned. With a slotted spoon, transfer to paper towels to drain. Pour off all but 2 tablespoons of fat from the skillet.

2. Add the onion to the skillet and cook, stirring often, until softened, about 5 minutes. Remove from the heat and stir in the flour.

3. In a 3 1/2-quart slow cooker, combine the potatoes and cooked onion. Pour in the clam juice, water, thyme, bay leaf, and pepper. Cover and slow-cook until the potatoes are tender, 6 to 7 hours on low (200°F).

4. Stir in the shrimp and heavy cream. Increase the heat to high (300°F) and cook just until the shrimp turn pink and firm, about 15 minutes. Remove the bay leaf and season with salt to taste. Spoon the soup into individual bowls, and sprinkle each serving with parsley.

Big Apple Scallop Chowder

While Yankee fishermen wouldn't consider anything that didn't have cream in it a chowder, Manhattanites insist that their tomato-based soup is just as much a chowder. For an unorthodox but unbeatable embellishment, float a shot of vodka in each serving.

Makes 4 to 6 servings

1. In a large skillet, heat the butter over medium heat. Add the onion, celery, carrot, and bell pepper. Cook, stirring often, until the onion is softened, about 5 minutes. Transfer to a 3½-quart slow cooker.

2. Stir the potatoes, the tomatoes with their purée, the clam juice, wine, water, thyme, bay leaf, and pepper into the slow cooker, breaking up the tomatoes with the side of a spoon. Cover and slow-cook until all the vegetables are tender, 6 to 7 hours on low (200°F).

3. Stir in the scallops. Increase the heat to high (300°F), cover, and cook until the scallops are firm, about 15 minutes. Discard the bay leaf and season the chowder with salt to taste.

4. Spoon the soup into individual bowls, and sprinkle each serving with basil.

2 tablespoons unsalted butter

1 medium onion, chopped

2 medium celery ribs, cut into ½-inch cubes

1 medium carrot, cut into ½-inch cubes

1 medium green bell pepper, seeded and cut into ½-inch cubes

2 medium boiling potatoes, scrubbed, unpeeled, and cut into ½-inch cubes

1 28-ounce can peeled tomatoes in thick tomato purée

2 cups bottled clam juice

1 cup dry white wine

1 cup water

1 teaspoon dried thyme

1 bay leaf

¼ teaspoon freshly ground black pepper

1 pound bay scallops, cut into 1-inch pieces if large

Salt to taste

Chopped fresh basil or parsley, for garnish

Salmon, Mushroom, and Pea Chowder

This ivory-colored broth is accented with pale-pink chunks of salmon and beige mushroom slices and sprinkled with bright green peas. If you're feeling flush, substitute fresh wild mushrooms for the ordinary ones.

Makes 4 to 6 servings

1. In a large skillet, melt the butter over medium heat. Add the onion, celery, and mushrooms and cook until the mushrooms have given off their liquid and are beginning to brown, about 7 minutes.

2. In a 3½-quart slow cooker, combine the cooked vegetables with the potatoes. Pour in the clam juice, water, wine, tarragon, thyme, and pepper. Cover and slow-cook until the potatoes are tender, 6 to 7 hours on low (200°F).

3. In a small bowl, whisk the cornstarch into the cream. Stir into the chowder, and add the salmon and peas. Increase the heat to high (300°F), cover, and cook until the salmon is firm, about 15 minutes. Taste the chowder and add salt to taste. Spoon the chowder in individual bowls, and sprinkle each serving with chives.

Whenever I make chowder, I add the salt at the end of the cooking time, rather than the beginning. Chowders have naturally salty ingredients, such as bacon, clam juice, and fish, and I wait for them to release all of their salt into the broth before seasoning.

2 tablespoons unsalted butter

1 medium onion, chopped

1 medium celery rib, cut into ½-inch-thick slices

10 ounces fresh mushrooms, sliced

2 medium boiling potatoes, scrubbed, unpeeled, and cut into ½-inch cubes

2 cups bottled clam juice

2 cups water

½ cup dry white wine

1 teaspoon dried tarragon

¼ teaspoon dried thyme

¼ teaspoon freshly ground white pepper

2 tablespoons cornstarch

½ cup heavy cream

1 pound salmon fillets, skinned and cut into 1-inch pieces

1 cup frozen petite peas, defrosted

Salt to taste

Minced fresh chives or chopped fresh parsley, for garnish

Athenian Shrimp in Tomato and Feta Sauce

Serve this Greek specialty spooned over hot cooked rice or orzo, a rice-shaped pasta.

Makes 4 to 6 servings

1. In a medium skillet, heat the oil over medium heat. Add the onion and garlic. Cook, stirring often, until the onion is softened, about 4 minutes. Transfer to a 3½-quart slow cooker.

2. Add the tomatoes with their purée, the tomato paste, wine, parsley, oregano, and pepper. Cover and slow-cook for 6 to 8 hours on low (200°F).

3. Increase the heat to high (300°F) and add the shrimp. Cook just until the shrimp are firm and have turned pink, about 15 minutes. Stir in the feta cheese, and serve immediately.

2 tablespoons olive oil

1 medium onion, chopped

1 garlic clove, minced

1 28-ounce can peeled tomatoes in thick tomato purée

1 6-ounce can tomato paste

¼ cup dry white wine or dry vermouth

2 tablespoons chopped fresh parsley

1 teaspoon dried oregano

¼ teaspoon freshly ground black pepper

1½ pounds medium shrimp, peeled and deveined

2 ounces feta cheese, cut into ¼-inch cubes

Seafood Etouffé

Seafood Etouffé is as New Orleans as a Dixieland band. Like most Creole dishes, the sauce features the "holy quintet" of seasoning vegetables: onions, scallions, green peppers, celery, and garlic. In the Crescent City, Seafood Etouffé would be served over rice, but you should also try it as a sauce for pasta.

Makes 4 to 6 servings

1. In a large skillet, heat the oil over medium heat. Add the onion, scallions, celery, bell and chile peppers, and garlic and cook, stirring often, until the onions are softened, about 6 minutes. Transfer to a 3 1/2-quart slow cooker. Add the tomatoes with their juice, tomato paste, salt, thyme, basil, oregano, and cayenne pepper, and break up the tomatoes with the side of a spoon.

2. Cover and slow-cook for 6 to 7 hours on low (200°F).

3. Increase the heat to high (300°F), and stir in the shrimp and scallops. Cook this until the seafood is firm, about 15 minutes. Stir in the cornstarch mixture and cook just until thickened. Sprinkle with the parsley and spoon over the hot rice or pasta.

2 tablespoons olive oil

1 medium onion, chopped

3 scallions, chopped

1 medium celery rib, cut into 1/2-inch-thick slices

1 medium green bell pepper, seeded and chopped

1 fresh hot green chile pepper, seeded and minced

2 garlic cloves, minced

3 15-ounce cans peeled Italian tomatoes, undrained

3 tablespoons tomato paste

1/2 teaspoon salt

1/2 teaspoon dried thyme

1/2 teaspoon dried basil

1/2 teaspoon dried oregano

1/4 teaspoon cayenne pepper

12 ounces medium shrimp, peeled and deveined

12 ounces scallops, quartered if large

2 teaspoons cornstarch dissolved in 1 tablespoon water

2 tablespoons chopped parsley

4 cups hot freshly cooked rice or 1 pound cooked pasta

North Beach Cioppino

Cioppino is a full-flavored fish stew made popular in the Italian restaurants of San Francisco. During my college days in that town, my friends and I frequented an inexpensive restaurant in North Beach that served cioppino by the bucket. I still enjoy it often, usually by itself with crusty sourdough bread, but sometimes spooned into individual bowls over hot cooked spaghetti.

Makes 4 to 6 servings

1. In a large skillet, heat the oil over medium heat. Add the onion and celery and cook, stirring often, until the onion is softened, about 5 minutes. Add the garlic and cook, stirring often, for 1 minute. Transfer to a 3½-quart slow cooker.

2. Stir in the clam juice, water, tomatoes with their juice, the red wine, parsley, basil, thyme, salt, red pepper, and bay leaf, breaking up the tomatoes with the side of a spoon. Cover and slow-cook for 4 to 5 hours on low (200°F).

3. Increase the heat to high (300°F) and stir in the snapper and shrimp. Cover and cook until just cooked through, about 15 minutes. Spoon into individual soup bowls and serve immediately.

Cioppino lends itself to improvisation. For example, you certainly can substitute dry white wine for red. Scallops can be used instead of, or in addition to, the shrimp. Cooked shelled crab, clams, or mussels should be stirred in just before serving, as they will heat sufficiently in the hot broth. If red snapper is unavailable, use any other non-oily white fish, such as sea bass or cod, but avoid oily fish like bluefish, whiting, or salmon.

2 tablespoons olive oil

1 medium onion, chopped

2 medium celery ribs, chopped

2 garlic cloves, minced

4 cups bottled clam juice

1 cup water

1 28-ounce can peeled Italian tomatoes, undrained

1 cup dry red wine, such as Zinfandel

2 tablespoons chopped fresh parsley

1 teaspoon dried basil

1 teaspoon dried thyme

½ teaspoon salt

¼ teaspoon crushed hot red pepper

1 bay leaf

1 pound red snapper fillets, skinned and cut into 1-inch pieces

½ pound medium shrimp, peeled and deveined

Soupe de Poissons

Smooth, golden-hued fish soup is another dish I learned to love when touring the Cote d'Azur. It is a refined relation of the more raffish bouillabaisse, and I find it is a faultless opener to a celebratory meal. (It is the traditional first course at my Christmas Eve supper.) Use two different kinds of fish to create a complexity of flavor. Sea bass, cod, porgy, and tilefish all are excellent, but do not use oily fish like salmon or mackerel.

Makes 4 to 6 servings

1. In a medium skillet, heat 1 tablespoon of the oil over low heat. Add the onion, chopped fennel, and garlic. Cover tightly and cook until the vegetables are softened, about 10 minutes. Transfer to a 3½-quart slow cooker.

2. Stir in the clam juice, tomatoes with their juice, the white wine, parsley, thyme, savory, salt, fennel seed, and hot pepper, breaking up the tomatoes with the side of the spoon. Cover and slow-cook until the vegetables are very tender, 4 to 5 hours on low (200°F).

3. Increase the heat to high (300°F) and add the fish and saffron. Cover and cook until the fish is cooked through, about 15 minutes. Using a slotted spoon, transfer the solids, including the fish, to a food processor and purée. Stir the purée back into the cooking liquid.

4. Meanwhile, preheat the oven to 400°F. Place the bread slices on a baking sheet and brush with the remaining 3 tablespoons oil.

¼ cup extra-virgin olive oil, divided

1 large onion, chopped

1 small fennel bulb (about 9 ounces), chopped

2 garlic cloves, minced

4 cups bottled clam juice

1 15-ounce can peeled Italian tomatoes, undrained

1 cup dry white wine

2 tablespoons chopped fresh parsley

1 teaspoon dried thyme

½ teaspoon dried savory

½ teaspoon salt

¼ teaspoon fennel seed, crushed

¼ teaspoon crushed hot red pepper

1 pound striped bass fillets

1 pound red snapper fillets, skinned, cut into 1-inch pieces

1 teaspoon crushed saffron threads

Bake until toasted, 12 to 15 minutes. (The toasted bread can be prepared up to 8 hours ahead and kept at room temperature.)

5. Place a piece of toasted bread in the bottom of each soup bowl, and spoon the soup into the bowls. Pass bowls of grated cheese and Aïoli.

8 slices French or Italian bread

Freshly grated imported Parmesan cheese

Aïoli (recipe follows)

Aïoli

This spicy, garlicky mayonnaise (pronounced "eye-OH-lee") is an essential condiment for Soupe de Poissons. Any leftover can be used as a sandwich spread or a dip for crudités. I use a blender for easy preparation. Don't think that using all extra-virgin olive oil will make a better sauce—it will only make it unappetizingly heavy.

Makes about 1½ cups

1 large egg, at room temperature

4 garlic cloves, crushed

1 teaspoon lemon juice

¼ teaspoon crushed saffron threads

¼ teaspoon salt

¼ teaspoon crushed hot red pepper

¾ cup extra-virgin olive oil

¾ cup vegetable oil

1. In a blender, combine the egg, garlic, lemon juice, saffron, salt, and red pepper and pulse to blend. In a glass measuring cup, combine the olive and vegetable oils.

2. With the motor running, slowly add the oils to the egg mixture, blending until thickened. (The aïoli can be prepared up to 1 day ahead, covered, and refrigerated. Remove from the refrigerator 1 hour before serving.)

When making aïoli, be sure all the ingredients are at room temperature. If the sauce does separate, place a tablespoon of prepared Dijon mustard in a small bowl. Gradually add the broken sauce, whisking constantly until the aïoli is once again smooth and thick.

Snapper, Oyster, and Ham Gumbo

Gumbo, that Cajun soup so thick you almost eat it with a fork, can be composed of almost anything that flies, walks, or swims. I like a recipe that has a little of everything, such as this one with snapper, ham, and oysters. Roux, the flour-and-oil mixture that gives authentic gumbo its distinctive color and flavor, is almost as tricky to make as wrestlin' a 'gator, but if you cook it over medium heat and whisk constantly, it will brown without scorching.

Makes 6 to 8 servings

1. In a large skillet, heat the oil over medium-high heat until almost smoking. Gradually whisk in the flour and reduce the heat to medium. Cook, whisking constantly, until the mixture is nut brown, about 4 minutes. Add the ham, onion, celery, green pepper, and scallions and cook, stirring often, until the vegetables are softened, about 5 minutes. Add the okra and garlic and cook for 2 minutes. Transfer to a 3½-quart slow cooker.

2. Add the water, clam juice, tomatoes with their juice, the salt, thyme, basil, bay leaves, cayenne, and black pepper, and break up the tomatoes with the side of a spoon. Cover and slow-cook until the okra is very tender, 5 to 6 hours on low (200°F).

3. Increase the heat to high (300°F). Add the snapper, oysters, and reserved oyster juices and cook just until the oysters curl at the edges, about 15 minutes.

4. To serve, place a large spoonful of rice in each soup bowl and ladle the gumbo over the rice.

½ cup vegetable oil

½ cup all-purpose flour

6 ounces smoked ham, cut into ½-inch cubes (about 1 cup)

1 medium onion, chopped

1 medium celery rib, chopped

1 medium green bell pepper, seeded and chopped

4 scallions, chopped

12 ounces okra, in ½-inch slices

3 garlic cloves, minced

3 cups water

2 cups bottled clam juice

1 15-ounce can peeled tomatoes, undrained

1 teaspoon salt

1 teaspoon dried thyme

½ teaspoon dried basil

2 bay leaves

¼ teaspoon cayenne pepper

¼ teaspoon black pepper

1 pound red snapper fillets, skinned, cut into 1-inch pieces

16 oysters, shucked, juices reserved

4 cups hot freshly cooked rice

Farmers' Market Lobster and Corn Chowder

Each summer, the produce in my local farmers' market is so irresistibly gorgeous that I always come home with an embarrassment of groceries. This soup was created one morning when my refrigerator was bulging with summer's bounty. Substitute eight ounces cooked chopped clams for the lobster if you like.

Makes 4 to 6 servings

1. In a 3½-quart slow cooker, layer the vegetables in the following order: potatoes, corn, zucchini, bell pepper, onion, and chile pepper. Add in the clam juice, butter, savory, and pepper. Cover and slow-cook until the vegetables are tender, 5 to 6 hours on low (200°F).

2. Using a slotted spoon, transfer about 1 cup of the cooked vegetables to a blender and purée until smooth. Stir the puréed vegetables back into the slow cooker. Increase the heat to high (300°F). Add the half-and-half and cook until the soup is hot, about 1 hour.

3. Stir in the lobster and tomatoes and cook just until heated through, about 10 minutes. Taste the chowder and add salt to taste. Serve the soup in individual soup bowls, and sprinkle each serving with some of the scallions.

4 medium boiling potatoes, scrubbed, unpeeled, and cut into ½-inch rounds

1½ cups fresh (from 3 ears) or frozen corn kernels

2 medium zucchini, cut into ½-inch-thick rounds

1 medium red bell pepper, seeded and chopped

1 small onion, chopped

1 fresh hot green chile pepper (such as jalapeño), seeded and minced

2 cups bottled clam juice

2 tablespoons unsalted butter

1 teaspoon dried savory

¼ teaspoon freshly ground white pepper

2 cups half-and-half

1 pound cooked lobster, cut into 1-inch pieces

2 large ripe tomatoes, seeded and chopped

salt, to taste

2 scallions, finely chopped

Scallop, Shrimp, and Sausage Jambalaya

Another Creole shellfish dish, cooked with herbed, tomato-flavored rice, and studded with spicy sausage.

Makes 6 servings

1. In a large skillet, heat the oil over medium heat. Add the onion, celery, and bell pepper and cook, stirring often, until the onion is softened, about 5 minutes. Add the rice and garlic and cook, stirring constantly, for 1 minute. Transfer the mixture to a 3½-quart slow cooker.

2. Add the tomato juice, clam juice, water, Worcestershire sauce, thyme, oregano, salt, black and cayenne peppers. Cover and slow-cook until the rice is barely tender, 5 to 6 hours on low (200°F).

3. Meanwhile, in a medium skillet over medium heat, cook the sausage, turning often, until browned, about 5 minutes.

4. During the last 15 minutes of cooking, stir the sausage, shrimp, and scallops into the jambalaya. Increase the heat to high (300°F), cover, and cook just until the shellfish are firm. Serve immediately.

2 tablespoons olive oil

1 medium onion, chopped

1 medium celery rib, chopped

1 medium red bell pepper, seeded and chopped

1 cup converted long-grain rice

2 garlic cloves, minced

1½ cups tomato juice

1 cup bottled clam juice

1 cup water

1 tablespoon Worcestershire sauce

½ teaspoon dried thyme

½ teaspoon dried oregano

½ teaspoon salt

¼ teaspoon freshly ground black pepper

¼ teaspoon cayenne pepper

8 ounces andouille or kielbasa sausage, cut into ½-inch-thick rounds

8 ounces medium shrimp, peeled and deveined

8 ounces scallops, halved if large

Slow-Cooked Beans

Have you ever seen old-fashioned bean pots? They're made out of crockery, they're taller than they are wide, and . . . well, they look pretty much like slow cooker inserts.

If the best beans are slowly cooked in crockery, it should be no surprise that a slow cooker makes fabulous beans. However, there are a few hints to keep in mind for successful bean cuisine.

· All beans are different, and their size and age is reflected in their cooking time. Be flexible with your cooking times.

· Beans have certain enzymes that make them difficult for some people to digest. This problem can be reduced by presoaking the beans, as some of these enzymes leach out into the soaking water, which is discarded. You can slow-cook beans without presoaking, but it takes a good ten to fourteen hours to get them soft. Besides, as the presoaking makes them so much easier to digest, there's no reason to skip this step.

· There are two ways to presoak dried beans:

To soak the beans overnight, place the beans in a large bowl and add enough cold water to cover the beans by 2 inches. Let the beans stand at room temperature overnight (or for at least 8 hours). Drain the beans well before proceeding. The overnight soaking method is the better way of soaking beans, as they then seem to cook more evenly.

To quick-soak the beans, place the beans in a large pot, and add enough water to cover by 2 inches. Bring to a boil over high heat, and boil for 2 minutes. Remove from the heat, cover, and let stand for 1 hour. Drain the beans well.

· Regardless of the presoaking method, most recipes call for beans to be cooked further in a saucepan until just tender before combining them in the slow cooker with other ingredients. Most recipes—but beans can be cooked in a slow cooker if there are no tomatoes or sugar (which have a toughening effect on beans) included as ingredients. (Salt is also a bean toughener, so add it toward the end of the cooking time.) To precook beans, place the soaked, drained beans in a large pot and add fresh water to cover by 2 inches. Bring to a boil over high heat, then reduce the heat to low and simmer until the beans are just tender. Remember, the cooking times will change with each variety of bean, and even from bag to bag of the same variety.

Orangey Rosemary Beans

Orange and rosemary may sound like an odd combination, but these slightly sweet beans are perfect alongside a baked ham at a buffet. Serve them right out of the slow cooker, which will keep the beans warm for hours.

Makes 6 to 8 servings

1. In a large pot, combine the beans and enough cold water to cover by 2 inches. Bring to a boil over high heat, and boil for 2 minutes. Remove from heat, cover the pot, and let stand for 1 hour; drain well. (The beans can also be soaked overnight in a large bowl with enough water to cover by 2 inches, then drained.)

2. Return the beans to the pot and add enough fresh water to cover by 2 inches. Bring to a boil over high heat, reduce the heat to low, and simmer until the beans are almost tender, about 40 minutes. Drain, reserving 2 cups of the cooking liquid. (The beans can be prepared up to 1 day ahead; cover and refrigerate the beans and the cooking liquid separately.)

3. In a 3½-quart slow cooker, combine the reserved 2 cups cooking liquid, the onion, marmalade, brown sugar, mustard, rosemary, salt, and pepper. Stir in the drained beans. Cover and slow-cook until the beans are very tender, 8 to 9 hours on low (200°F). During the last hour of cooking, increase the heat to high (300°F) and uncover to evaporate excess liquid.

1 pound dried Great Northern beans, rinsed, drained, and picked over

1 medium onion, chopped

½ cup orange marmalade

⅓ cup packed brown sugar

1 tablespoon Dijon mustard

1 teaspoon dried rosemary

½ teaspoon salt

¼ teaspoon freshly ground black pepper

Very Nice Red Beans and Rice

In New Orleans, long-simmered red beans, ham, and rice are the traditional Monday night meal. I'll make these any day of the week.

Makes 6 to 8 servings

1. In a large pot, combine the beans with enough cold water to cover by 2 inches. Bring to a boil over high heat, and boil for 2 minutes. Remove from the heat, cover the pot, and let stand for 1 hour; drain well. (The beans can also be soaked overnight in a large bowl with enough water to cover by 2 inches, then drained.)

2. In a large skillet, heat the oil over medium-high heat. Add the celery, onion, bell pepper, scallions, and garlic. Cook, stirring often, until the onions are softened, about 6 minutes. Transfer to a 3½-quart slow cooker.

3. Stir in the drained beans, water, beef broth, and red pepper. Bury the ham hock in the bean mixture. Cover and slow-cook until the beans are very tender, 9 to 10 hours on low (200°F).

4. Remove the ham hock, and pull off and discard the fat and skin. Remove the meat from the bone and coarsely chop. Return the meat to the pot, and stir in the salt.

5. Serve the beans in bowls, spooned over hot cooked rice, and sprinkled with chopped scallions.

Variation: *One smoked turkey wing (about 1 pound), chopped into 2-inch pieces, can be substituted for the ham hock.*

1 pound dried small red chili beans, rinsed, drained, and picked over

2 tablespoons vegetable oil

3 celery ribs, chopped

1 medium onion, chopped

1 medium green bell pepper, seeded and chopped

3 scallions, chopped

2 garlic cloves, minced

3⅓ cups water

2⅔ cups double-strength beef broth

½ teaspoon crushed red hot pepper

1 smoked ham hock (about 9 ounces), skin scored in a diamond pattern with a sharp knife

1 teaspoon salt

4 cups hot cooked rice

Chopped scallions, for garnish

Lentil-Tomato Stew

A tomatoey legume stew is delicious in its original meatless form, or with the sausage variation outlined at the end of the recipe.

1. In a 3½-quart slow cooker, combine the water, tomatoes with their juice, the tomato paste, red wine, basil, thyme, and crushed red pepper. Break up the tomatoes with a wooden spoon, and stir to blend in the tomato paste. Add the lentils, onion, carrots, celery, and garlic.

2. Cover and cook until the lentils are tender, 10 to 12 hours on low (200°F), 4 to 5 hours on high (300°F). Stir in the salt.

3. Serve the stew in bowls, sprinkled with chopped basil.

Sausage and Lentil Stew: *Position a broiler rack about 4 inches from the source of heat and preheat the broiler. Broil 1 pound fresh Italian sausages (pricked all over with a fork), turning often, until well browned on all sides, about 15 minutes. Cut the sausages into 1-inch chunks and stir into the stew just before serving.*

3 cups water

1 28-ounce can peeled Italian tomatoes, undrained

1 6-ounce can tomato paste

½ cup dry red wine, such as Zinfandel

¾ teaspoon dried basil

¾ teaspoon dried thyme

½ teaspoon crushed hot red pepper

1 pound dried lentils, rinsed, drained, and picked over

1 large onion, chopped

4 medium carrots, cut into ½-inch rounds

4 medium celery ribs, cut into ½-inch-thick slices

3 garlic cloves, minced

1 teaspoon salt

Chopped fresh basil or parsley, for garnish

Frijoles Gorditos

When I was a language student in Guadalajara, we used to have these for breakfast. In Mexico, we were served *frijoles* as a side dish, but I think you'll find them hearty enough for a main course. Don't add salt and red pepper until the end of the cooking time, as different brands of sausage will lend variable amounts of salt and spiciness to the broth.

Makes 6 to 8 servings

1. In a large pot, combine the beans and enough cold water to cover by 2 inches. Bring to a boil over high heat, and boil for 2 minutes. Remove from the heat, cover the pot, and let stand for 1 hour; drain well. (The beans can also be soaked overnight in a large bowl with enough water to cover by 2 inches, then drained.)

2. Return the beans to the pot and add enough fresh water to cover by 2 inches. Bring to a boil over high heat, reduce the heat to low, and simmer until the beans are barely tender, about 45 minutes. Drain, reserving 3 cups of the cooking liquid. (The beans can be prepared 1 day ahead; cover and refrigerate the beans and the cooking liquid separately.)

3. In a large skillet over medium heat, cook the chorizo, onion, garlic, and chile pepper, stirring often, until the onion is softened and the sausage is sizzling, about 5 minutes. Stir in the oregano, marjoram, and red pepper.

4. In a 3½-quart slow cooker, combine the drained beans, the

1 pound dried pink beans, rinsed, drained, and picked over

12 ounces chorizo sausage (or other spicy smoked sausage), cut into 3/4-inch-thick rounds

1 small onion, chopped

2 garlic cloves, minced

1 fresh hot green chile pepper (such as jalapeño), seeded and minced

1/4 teaspoon dried oregano

1/4 teaspoon dried marjoram

1/4 teaspoon crushed hot red pepper

1/2 teaspoon salt

reserved 3 cups cooking liquid, and the chorizo mixture. Cover and slow-cook until the beans are very tender, 8 to 10 hours on low (200°F).

5. Skim the fat from the surface of the beans. Stir in the salt. Using a large spoon, crush enough of the beans against the sides of the slow cooker to thicken the beans to desired consistency. (Some prefer these beans soupy, but I like them thick.)

Hoppin' John

Down South, black-eyed peas mean good luck, and many New Year's Day parties feature a big pot of this boldly spiced pea and sausage dish with a penny buried in it. Whoever is served the coin will be especially lucky during the year. Normally, the rice is cooked right with the peas, but I find the results much lighter if the rice is cooked separately and served as a bed for the soupy stew.

Makes 8 servings

1 pound dried black-eyed peas, rinsed, drained, and picked over

1 tablespoon vegetable oil

2 medium onions, chopped

2 medium celery ribs, chopped

2 garlic cloves, minced

5 cups water

2²⁄₃ cups double-strength beef broth, homemade or canned

1 teaspoon crushed hot red pepper

1 teaspoon dried thyme

½ teaspoon dried basil

½ teaspoon dried oregano

1 pound bulk pork sausage

1 teaspoon salt

4 cups hot cooked rice

1. In a large pot, combine the black-eyed peas with enough cold water to cover by 2 inches. Bring to a boil over high heat, and boil for 2 minutes. Remove from the heat, cover the pot, and let stand for 1 hour; drain well. (The black-eyed peas can also be soaked overnight in a large bowl with enough water to cover by 2 inches, then drained.) Place the peas in a 3½-quart slow cooker.

2. In a large skillet, heat the oil over medium-high heat. Add the onions and celery and cook, stirring often, until the onions are softened, about 4 minutes. Add the garlic and stir for 1 minute. Stir the cooked vegetables into the black-eyed peas. Add the water, beef broth, crushed red pepper, thyme, basil, and oregano. Cover and slow-cook until the peas are tender, 7 to 8 hours on low (200°F).

3. Meanwhile, in a large skillet over medium heat, cook the sausage, stirring often to break up lumps, until cooked through, about 8 minutes. Drain off excess fat.

4. Stir the salt into the black-eyed peas, stir in the cooked sausage, and serve immediately, spooned over bowls of hot rice.

White Beans with Sage and Garlic

Cannellini, tender white kidney beans, heady with the perfume of sage and garlic, are an ever-present side dish on the tables of Tuscany. According to my friend Michele Scicolone, the author of *The Antipasto Table,* cannellini should never be quick-soaked, or they will end up as overcooked mush. So, plan ahead, follow her advice, use the slow cooker, and get superlative results.

Makes 4 to 6 servings

1 pound dried cannellini (white kidney beans), rinsed, drained, and picked over

1 garlic clove, crushed

2 fresh sage leaves, minced, or 1/4 teaspoon crushed dried sage

1 teaspoon salt

1 tablespoon extra-virgin olive oil

1. In a large bowl, combine the beans and add enough cold water to cover by 2 inches. Let stand at room temperature overnight. Drain well and place in a 3 1/2-quart slow cooker.

2. Add the garlic, sage, and enough cold water to cover by 2 inches. Cover and slow-cook until the beans are just tender, 6 to 7 hours on low (200°F). During the last 30 minutes of cooking, stir in the salt.

3. If necessary, drain the beans. Serve hot, warm, or at room temperature, drizzled with the olive oil.

Cassoulet

Cassoulet, a complex French stew of beans, lamb, and pork, and often duck or goose as well, is as sturdy as it is delicious. Traditional recipes make enough for an army, but my version serves a manageable group. It is important to use the quick-soaking method for the beans, which will soften them more than an overnight soak. Otherwise, your meat may be overdone by the time the beans are tender.

Makes 6 to 8 servings

1. In a large pot, combine the beans and enough cold water to cover by 2 inches. Bring to a boil over high heat, and boil for 2 minutes. Remove from the heat, cover the pot, and let stand for 1 hour; drain well.

2. Return the beans to the pot and add enough fresh water to cover by 2 inches. Bring to a boil over high heat, reduce the heat to low, and simmer until tender, 30 to 40 minutes. Drain well. Transfer to a 3½-quart slow cooker.

3. In a medium saucepan, cover the bacon cubes with cold water. Bring to a simmer over medium-low heat, and simmer for 2 minutes. Drain, rinse well under cold running water, and pat dry with paper towels.

4. In a large skillet, heat the oil over medium heat. Add the bacon cubes and cook, turning often, until browned. Using a slotted spoon, transfer the bacon to paper towels to drain.

5. Increase the heat to medium-high. In batches without crowd-

1 pound dried Great Northern beans, rinsed, drained, and picked over

4 ounces slab bacon, skin removed, cut into ½-inch cubes

1 tablespoon vegetable oil, plus more if needed

1½ pounds boneless lamb shoulder, well trimmed and cut into 2-inch pieces

1½ pounds boneless pork shoulder, well trimmed and cut into 2-inch pieces

½ teaspoon salt

¼ teaspoon freshly ground black pepper

1 large onion, chopped

2 garlic cloves, minced

¾ cup water

2 tablespoons tomato paste

2 tablespoons chopped fresh parsley

1 teaspoon dried thyme

1 bay leaf

ing, cook the lamb and pork in the bacon fat remaining in the pan, turning often, until browned, about 5 minutes. Using a slotted spoon, transfer the meat to a plate and season with the salt and pepper. Stir the meat and bacon into the beans.

6. Add the onion to the skillet, adding more oil if necessary. Reduce the heat to medium and cook, stirring often, until softened, about 5 minutes. Add the garlic and cook, stirring often, for 1 minute. Add the water, tomato paste, parsley, thyme, and bay leaf and bring to a simmer, scraping up the browned bits on the bottom of the pan with a wooden spoon. Add the mixture to the beans.

7. Pour in the chicken broth and wine, and stir well. Cover and slow-cook until the beans are tender, 6 to 7 hours on low (200°F). During the last hour of cooking, stir in the sausage rounds.

8. In a large skillet, melt the butter over medium-high heat. Add the bread crumbs and cook, stirring often, until lightly browned, 3 to 5 minutes. Sprinkle the browned crumbs on top of the cassoulet and serve directly from the slow cooker.

1 cup double-strength chicken broth, canned or homemade

½ cup dry white wine or dry vermouth

1 pound kielbasa, cut into ½-inch-thick rounds

2 tablespoons unsalted butter

1 cup fresh bread crumbs

Sugarbush Beans

These are inspired by an old Vermont recipe in which the baked beans are sweetened with local maple syrup. Salt pork and prepared mustard give them a notable old-fashioned flavor. Be sure your beans are par-cooked before mixing with the other ingredients!

Makes 12 servings

1. In a large pot, combine the beans and enough water to cover by 2 inches. Bring to a boil over high heat, and boil for 2 minutes. Remove from the heat, cover the pot, and let stand for 1 hour. Drain well. (The beans can also be soaked overnight in a large bowl with enough cold water to cover by 2 inches, then drained.)

2. Return the beans to the pot and add enough fresh water to cover by 2 inches. Add the halved onion and bring to a boil over high heat. Reduce the heat to low and simmer until the beans are almost tender, about 1 hour. Drain well, reserving 1 cup of the cooking liquid. Discard the onion. (The beans can be prepared a day ahead; cover and refrigerate the beans and the cooking liquid separately.)

3. In a 3½-quart slow cooker, combine the salt pork, reserved 1 cup cooking liquid, the chopped onion, maple syrup, spicy mustard, catsup, and dry mustard. Stir in the drained beans. Cover and slow-cook until the beans are just tender, 7 to 8 hours on low (200°F).

4. Increase the heat to high (300°F), uncover, and cook until the excess liquid has evaporated, about 1 hour.

2 pounds dried Great Northern beans, rinsed, drained, and picked over

2 large onions, 1 halved and the other chopped

6 ounces salt pork, rind removed, cut into ½-inch cubes

1 cup pure maple syrup or pancake syrup

¼ cup prepared spicy brown mustard

¼ cup catsup

2 tablespoons dry mustard

White Bean, Tuna, and Tomato Salad

This is one of my favorite main-course bean salads, and I make it many times throughout the summer. It can be endlessly improvised on, substituting cubed Italian salami for the tuna, for example, or fresh sage for the basil.

Makes 6 to 8 servings

1. In a large bowl, combine the cannellini and enough cold water to cover by 2 inches. Let stand at room temperature overnight, then drain well. (Do not use the quick-soak method.)

2. Place the drained beans in a 3 ½-quart slow cooker and add enough fresh cold water to cover by 2 inches. Cover and slow-cook until the beans are just tender, 5 to 6 hours on low (200°F). During the last 30 minutes, stir in 1 teaspoon of the salt. Drain the beans well and cool until tepid, about 30 minutes.

3. Place the beans in a bowl and toss gently with the tuna, tomatoes, and red onion.

4. In a medium bowl, whisk the vinegar with the remaining ½ teaspoon salt, the garlic, and pepper. Gradually whisk in the oil. Pour the dressing over the beans, sprinkle with the basil, and toss gently. Cover and refrigerate for at least 1 hour before serving. (The salad can be prepared up to 1 day ahead, covered, and refrigerated. One hour before serving, remove from the refrigerator and adjust the seasoning as necessary with vinegar, oil, salt, and pepper.)

As bean salads chill, they continue to soak up the dressing, making it necessary to reseason them before serving.

1 pound dried cannellini (white kidney beans), rinsed, drained, and picked over

1½ teaspoons salt, divided

2 6½-ounce cans tuna packed in water, drained and flaked

4 medium plum tomatoes (about 8 ounces), cut into ½-inch cubes

1 small red onion, finely chopped

3 tablespoons red wine vinegar

2 garlic cloves, minced

¼ teaspoon freshly ground black pepper

¾ cup extra-virgin olive oil

3 tablespoons finely chopped fresh basil

Black Bean, Sweet Pepper, and Goat Cheese Salad

An eye-opening salad, dramatically colored with a confetti of minced red, yellow, and green sweet and hot peppers against a backdrop of black beans. This is a perfect partner for grilled lamb kebabs. Soft goat cheese, such as chèvre, is best, but use feta cheese if necessary.

Makes 6 to 8 servings

1 pound dried black beans, rinsed, drained, and picked over

1 large onion, halved

1½ teaspoons salt, divided

6 scallions, finely chopped

3 bell peppers (1 red, 1 yellow, and 1 green), seeded and finely chopped

1 fresh hot green chile pepper (such as jalapeño), seeded and minced

3 tablespoons lime juice

1 garlic clove, minced

¼ teaspoon freshly ground black pepper

¾ cup olive oil

3 tablespoons chopped fresh cilantro or basil

6 ounces soft goat cheese (chèvre), crumbled

1. In a large pot, combine the beans with enough cold water to cover by 2 inches. Bring to a boil over high heat, and boil for 2 minutes. Remove from the heat, cover, and let stand for 1 hour. Drain well.

2. Place the drained beans and the onion in a 3½-quart slow cooker and add enough fresh cold water to cover by 2 inches. Cover and slow-cook until the beans are just tender, 5 to 6 hours on low (200°F) or 2 to 3 hours on high (300°F). During the last 30 minutes, stir in 1 teaspoon of the salt. Drain the beans well, discard the onion, and cool until tepid, about 30 minutes.

3. Place the beans in a bowl and toss gently with the scallions and the bell and hot peppers.

4. In a medium bowl, whisk the lime juice with the remaining ½ teaspoon salt, garlic, and the pepper. Gradually whisk in the oil. Pour the dressing over the bean mixture, sprinkle with the cilantro, and toss gently. Cover and refrigerate for at least 1 hour before serving. (The salad can be prepared up to 1 day ahead, covered, and refrigerated. One hour before serving, remove from the refrigerator and adjust the seasonings as necessary with lime juice, oil, salt, and pepper.)

5. Just before serving, sprinkle with the cheese and toss gently.

Variation: *Turn this into a main-course salad by adding 3 cups chopped cooked lamb, beef, or chicken.*

Stews

For a satisfying, comforting culinary experience, few examples surpass sitting down to an aromatic bowl of stew. And no kitchen appliance makes better stew than a slow cooker. Here are a few tips to guide you toward making perfect slow-cooked stews.

For beef stews, bottom round is my favorite cut of beef. Chuck, while tasty, has more fat. Rump, while lean, can be slightly dry after cooking. Expensive, tender cuts of meat, such as tenderloin, are best oven-roasted, and do not make good stews. Short ribs are delicious cooked in the slow cooker, but be sure to broil them first to remove excess fat.

Pork shoulder, or Boston butt, makes great stew, but be sure to trim off the outer layer of fat. This cut of meat is a bargain, and is usually sold as a large, bone-in roast. Cut off the meat from the bone, then cut the meat into 2-inch cubes. (Save the bone to make a flavorful soup.) Boneless pork loin can make good stew, but as it is more tender than shoulder, the cooking time is necessarily shortened by at least one hour. To make pork ribs in the slow cooker, use meaty country ribs. Regular spare ribs make an awkward fit in most slow cookers, and country ribs give heartier servings. Broil the ribs before adding to the slow cooker to brown and remove excess fat.

Lamb shoulder, boneless and well trimmed, is the cut of choice for lamb stew. Boneless leg of lamb is much more tender, and will cook in about four hours. (If using leg, cut the vegetables smaller than usual to be sure they are done at the same time as the cubes of meat. Follow this procedure for pork loin, too.) Lamb shanks shine in the slow cooker, but have the butcher cut them crosswise into 2-inch-thick pieces so they will fit easily into the crockery insert.

Veal stew meat is usually boneless veal shoulder. Veal is leaner than other meats, so it doesn't need to be as well trimmed as the other meats, but you will want to cut away any extraneous tendons and connective tissue. Veal shank (osso buco) is normally sold sawed into 2-inch-thick pieces and will fit into the slow cooker without any trouble.

Be sure your stew meat is well trimmed so fat doesn't melt out into the cooking liquid. A high proportion of fat in the cooking liquid will raise its temperature above that of a leaner liquid. (Fat has a higher boiling temperature than water.) Then even if the slow cooker thermostat is turned to low, the cooking liquid could boil, and the stew meat would be overcooked.

Bistro Beef Bourguignon

Boeuf bourguignon is possibly the most famous beef stew in the world, and the slow cooker allows the flavors to mingle, making this version one of the best. A few steps are required to prepare the different ingredients for the slow cooker, but the extra effort makes for a perfect end result.

Makes 4 to 6 servings

1. Place the baby carrots and boiling onions in a 3½-quart slow cooker.

2. In a medium saucepan, combine the bacon and enough water to cover by 1 inch. Bring to a simmer over medium heat, and cook for 2 minutes. Drain well, rinse under cold running water, and pat dry with paper towels.

3. In a large skillet over medium heat, cook the bacon strips, turning often, until crisp and browned, about 5 minutes. Using a slotted spoon, transfer the bacon to paper towels to drain.

4. Increase the heat to medium-high. Add the beef, in batches without crowding, to the fat remaining in the pan and cook, turning often, until browned on all sides, about 5 minutes. Transfer the beef to the slow cooker, add the bacon, and season with the salt and pepper. Mix well, but leave the carrots and onions undisturbed.

5. Add the vegetable oil to the skillet and heat over medium heat. Add the mushrooms and shallots and cook, stirring often, until the mushrooms have given off their liquid and are beginning

1 pound baby carrots, peeled

1 pound small boiling onions, peeled (see page 97)

4 ounces slab bacon, rind removed, cut into 2- by ½-inch-wide strips

2 pounds boneless beef bottom round, cut into 2-inch pieces and well trimmed

1 teaspoon salt

¼ teaspoon freshly ground black pepper

1 tablespoon vegetable oil

10 ounces fresh mushrooms, quartered

4 shallots or scallions, finely chopped

2 garlic cloves, minced

½ cup dry red wine

¼ cup double-strength beef broth, canned or homemade

to brown, about 7 minutes. Add the garlic and stir for 30 seconds. Transfer the mushroom mixture to the slow cooker. Add the red wine, broth, parsley, tomato paste, thyme, and bay leaf to the skillet and bring to a simmer, stirring to blend in the tomato paste and scraping up the browned bits on the bottom of the skillet. Add to the slow cooker.

6. Cover and slow-cook until the beef is tender, 7 to 8 hours on low (200°F). With a slotted spoon, transfer the beef and vegetables to a serving bowl, discarding the bay leaf, and cover with foil to keep warm. Skim the fat from the surface of the cooking liquid.

7. In a medium skillet, melt the butter over low heat. Add the flour and cook, whisking constantly, without browning, for 1 minute. Whisk in the cooking liquid and bring to a boil. Cook, whisking often, until thickened and reduced to about 1¼ cups, about 10 minutes. Pour the sauce over the beef and vegetables, mix gently, and serve immediately.

The bacon is blanched before browning to remove excess salt. Do not skip this step, or your sauce may be too salty.

2 tablespoons chopped fresh parsley

1 tablespoon tomato paste

½ teaspoon dried thyme

1 bay leaf

2 tablespoons unsalted butter

2 tablespoons all-purpose flour

Daube de Boeuf

Daube de boeuf, the Provençal wine-marinated beef ragoût, is best when cooked in a tall crockery pot called a *daubière,* a vessel that allows the stew to cook slowly and develop flavor. (*Voilà!* A slow cooker!) Daubes are not made in a day, and this one, in fact, takes three to reach its full potential. It can be marinated, cooked, refrigerated, and then reheated in the same slow-cooker crockery insert. Daubes are different from other French stews in that the meat is often not browned and the cooking liquid is not turned into a separate sauce. Instead, the stew, with its unthickened (but slightly reduced), intensely flavored juices, is served over hot macaroni.

Makes 6 servings

1. In a 3½-quart slow-cooker crockery insert, combine the wine, onions, carrots, celery, garlic, parsley, tomatoes, olive oil, salt, thyme, basil, rosemary, pepper, and bay leaf. Add the beef and mix well. Cover with plastic wrap and refrigerate at least 4 hours or, preferably, overnight, stirring occasionally. Pour off and discard 1 cup of the marinade.

2. Slow-cook, covered, until the beef is tender, 7 to 8 hours on low (200°F). Remove the crockery insert from the slow cooker and cool the daube cool to room temperature. Cover with plastic wrap and refrigerate overnight to allow the flavors to mellow.

3. To reheat, preheat the oven to 350°F.

2 cups dry red wine, such as Zinfandel

2 medium onions, sliced

2 medium carrots, cut into ½-inch-thick rounds

2 medium celery ribs, cut into ½-inch-thick slices

4 garlic cloves, minced

2 tablespoons chopped fresh parsley

1 15-ounce can peeled Italian tomatoes, drained and chopped

2 tablespoons extra-virgin olive oil

1 teaspoon salt

1 teaspoon dried thyme

½ teaspoon dried basil

½ teaspoon dried rosemary

¼ teaspoon freshly ground black pepper

1 bay leaf

3 pounds boneless beef bottom round, well trimmed and cut into 2-inch pieces

½ cup black Mediterranean olives, pitted

Hot cooked macaroni

4.   Scrape off the fat from the surface of the daube. Cover the crockery insert with foil and bake for 30 minutes. Uncover and bake, stirring often, until the cooking liquid has reduced slightly and the meat is heated through, about 1 hour. During the last 10 minutes of baking, stir in the olives. Serve the daube over hot macaroni.

Bollito Misto

A true *bollito misto* is an elaborate Italian dish, in which entire meat roasts, whole sausages, and chickens are braised in a vegetable broth, then served with a piquant herb sauce. Few cooks, Italian or not, have a pot big enough to make old-fashioned *bollito misto*. However, the idea of a stew with lots of different meats is appealing, so I offer my version that is scaled down in volume, but not in flavor. Offer Garlic Mashed Potatoes (page 234) on the side, with some of the juices spooned over them.

Makes 8 servings

1. Season the beef and veal with the salt and pepper. In a 3½-quart slow cooker, combine the onions, carrots, and celery. Sprinkle with the parsley and add the bay leaf. Top with the meat, then pour in the water and broth. Cover and slow-cook until the meat is almost tender, 5 to 6 hours on low (200°F).

2. Increase the heat to high (300°F). Add the chicken breasts, cover, and cook until the chicken is cooked through, about 1 hour.

3. Meanwhile, in a medium skillet, combine the sausages with just enough cold water to cover. Bring to a simmer over medium heat, cover, and simmer until the sausages are cooked through, about 20 minutes. Remove from the heat and let the sausages stand in the water, covered, to keep warm.

4. When the meat is tender and the chicken breasts are done, drain the sausages, cut into 1-inch chunks, and stir into the stew.

1 pound boneless beef round, cut into 2-inch pieces and well trimmed

1 pound boneless veal stew meat, cut into 2-inch pieces and well trimmed

½ teaspoon salt

¼ teaspoon freshly ground black pepper

2 medium onions, quartered

3 medium carrots, cut into ½-inch-thick slices

3 medium celery ribs, cut into ½-inch-thick slices

2 tablespoons chopped fresh parsley

1 bay leaf

2¼ cups water

1⅔ cups double-strength beef or chicken broth, canned or homemade

4 chicken breast halves (about 1½ pounds), cut crosswise into halves

To serve, ladle into soup bowls, being sure that each guest gets a piece of chicken and some sausage, as well as beef and veal. Garnish each serving with a spoonful of herb sauce. Pass bowls of the remaining herb sauce and pickled vegetables on the side.

You will have plenty of leftover bollito misto cooking liquid; save it to use as a broth in other dishes. Cool the liquid to room temperature, then cover and refrigerate for up to 3 days, or freeze for up to 2 months. Remove the solidified fat on the surface before using.

4 fresh sweet or hot Italian sausages (about 4 ounces each), well pricked with a fork

Italian Green Herb Sauce (recipe follows)

Bottled pickled Italian vegetables (giardiniera), for garnish

Italian Green Herb Sauce

In addition to being the classic condiment for *bollito misto,* this pesto-like sauce goes well with cold roasts, too.

Makes about 2 cups

In a food processor or blender, combine the parsley, basil, nuts, mustard, lemon juice, garlic, and salt. With the machine running, slowly add the oil and process to form a smooth sauce. (The sauce can be made up to 2 days ahead, covered, and refrigerated. Remove from the refrigerator 1 hour before serving, and stir well to blend.)

1 1/2 cups packed fresh parsley leaves

1/4 cup chopped fresh basil or 2 teaspoons dried basil

1/2 cup pine nuts or walnuts

1 tablespoon Dijon mustard

1 tablespoon lemon juice

2 garlic cloves, crushed

1/2 teaspoon salt

1 1/3 cups extra-virgin olive oil

Beef Stroganoff

A delicious stew with a dilled sour-cream gravy that was put on this earth to be spooned over noodles.

Makes 4 to 6 servings

1. In a large skillet, heat the oil over medium-high heat. Add the beef, in batches without crowding, and cook, turning often, until browned on all sides. Transfer to a 3½-quart slow cooker. Season with the paprika, salt, and pepper and stir well.

2. Add the mushrooms and onions to the skillet, and add more oil if necessary. Reduce the heat to medium and cook, stirring often, until the mushrooms have given up their liquid and are beginning to brown, about 7 minutes. Add the beef broth and water, and stir to scrape up the browned bits on the bottom of the skillet. Transfer to the slow cooker.

3. Cover and slow-cook until the beef is tender, 7 to 8 hours on low (200°F). Using a slotted spoon, transfer the meat and vegetables to a serving bowl, and cover with aluminum foil to keep warm.

4. In a small bowl, whisk the cornstarch into the sour cream. Stir in the dill. Stir the sour cream mixture into the slow cooker and cook until the cooking liquid is slightly thickened, about 5 minutes. Pour the sauce over the meat and vegetables and mix gently. Serve immediately, spooning over the noodles.

When using only a portion of canned broth, freeze the remainder for another use.

2 tablespoons vegetable oil, plus more if needed

2½ pounds beef bottom round, cut into 2-inch cubes and well trimmed

1 teaspoon sweet Hungarian paprika

½ teaspoon salt

¼ teaspoon freshly ground black pepper

1 pound fresh mushrooms, sliced

2 medium onions, sliced

½ cup double-strength beef broth, canned or homemade

¼ cup water

1 tablespoon cornstarch

1 cup sour cream

2 tablespoons fresh dill or 1 teaspoon dried dill

Hot freshly cooked egg noodles

Portuguese Spiced Beef Stew *(Soupas)*

A Sunday afternoon visit to my godfather Frank's house often meant that his wife, Lorraine, would make *soupas,* a Portuguese beef stew that gets its tempting aroma from the addition of pickling spices.

Makes 4 to 6 servings

1. In a large skillet, heat the oil over medium-high heat. Add the beef cubes, in batches without crowding, and cook, turning occasionally, until browned on all sides, adding more oil if necessary. Transfer the beef cubes to a 3½-quart slow cooker and season with the salt and pepper.

2. Add more oil to the skillet, if necessary, and heat over medium heat. Add the onions and cook until softened, about 4 minutes. Add the garlic and stir for 1 minute. Stir in the red wine, tomato paste, pickling spices, and bay leaf. (You may prefer to place the pickling spices in a tea ball, or tie them up in a piece of rinsed cheesecloth, but I usually skip this refinement.) Bring to a simmer, scraping up the browned bits on the bottom of the skillet. Remove from the heat and stir in the tomatoes with their juices, breaking them up with the side of a spoon. Transfer the mixture to the slow cooker.

3. Cover and slow-cook until the meat is tender, 6 to 7 hours on low (200°F). Skim the fat from the surface of the stew and discard the bay leaf. If using dried mint, stir into the stew.

4. Place the bread chunks in a large serving bowl. Pour the stew over and let stand for 5 minutes. Sprinkle the stew with the fresh mint, if using, and serve immediately.

2 tablespoons olive oil, plus more if needed

2 pounds beef bottom round, cut into 2-inch pieces and well trimmed

½ teaspoon salt

¼ teaspoon freshly ground black pepper

2 medium onions, chopped

2 garlic cloves, minced

1 cup dry red wine, such as Zinfandel

1 6-ounce can tomato paste

1 tablespoon pickling spices

1 bay leaf

1 28-ounce can peeled Italian tomatoes, undrained

1 loaf Italian or French bread (about 7 ounces), torn into 3-inch chunks

2 tablespoons chopped fresh mint or 2 teaspoons dried mint

Farmhouse Beef and Vegetable Stew

Here's a no-frills, all-American stew with straightforward whole-someness. It's the ticket when you crave down-home comfort food.

Serves 4 to 6

1. In a large skillet, heat the oil over medium-high heat. Add the beef, in batches without crowding, and cook until browned, turning occasionally, and adding more oil if necessary. Transfer the browned meat to a plate, season with the salt and pepper, and set aside.

2. Add the beef broth, water, Worcestershire sauce, parsley, marjoram, thyme, and bay leaf to the skillet and bring to a boil, scraping up the browned bits on the bottom with a wooden spoon. Remove from the heat.

3. In a 3½-quart slow cooker, layer the vegetables in the following order: potatoes, turnips, carrots, onions, and celery. Add the beef cubes and their juices, then pour in the broth mixture.

4. Cover and cook until the meat is tender, 7 to 8 hours on low (200°F). Using a slotted spoon, transfer the meat and vegetables to a serving bowl, and cover with foil to keep warm. Skim the fat from the surface of the cooking liquid.

5. In a medium saucepan, melt the butter over medium heat. Add the flour and cook, whisking constantly, without browning, about 1 minute. Whisk in the cooking liquid. Bring to a simmer and cook, whisking often, until the sauce has reduced to about 1½

2 tablespoons vegetable oil, plus more if needed

2 pounds beef bottom round, cut into 2-inch cubes and well trimmed

½ teaspoon salt

¼ teaspoon freshly ground black pepper

1 cup double-strength beef broth, canned or homemade

¾ cup water

1 tablespoon Worcestershire sauce

2 tablespoons chopped fresh parsley

1 teaspoon dried marjoram

½ teaspoon dried thyme

1 bay leaf

2 medium boiling potatoes, scrubbed, unpeeled, and cut into ¾-inch cubes

2 medium turnips, scrubbed, unpeeled, and cut into ¾-inch cubes

2 large carrots, cut into ½-inch-thick rounds

cups, 8 to 10 minutes. Pour the sauce over the meat and vegetables, mix gently, and serve.

To peel boiling onions, blanch the onions in boiling water for 1 minute. Drain and rinse under cold running water. Using a small sharp knife, trim the top and bottom from each onion, and remove the peel. To prevent the onions from bursting during stewing, score the trimmed top and bottom of each one with a shallow "X."

12 small white boiling onions, peeled

1 medium celery rib, cut into ½-inch-thick slices

2 tablespoons unsalted butter

3 tablespoons all-purpose flour

Short Ribs with
Garden Patch Horseradish Sauce

Horseradish is one of the best things you can serve with short ribs, and its pungent presence is definitely felt in this sauce of puréed vegetables. Prepared horseradish loses its punch if opened and stored in the refrigerator too long, so be sure your bottle is fresh.

Makes 4 servings

1. Position a broiler rack 6 inches from the source of heat and preheat the broiler. Broil the short ribs, turning often, until browned on all sides, about 15 minutes. Transfer to a plate and season with the salt and pepper.

2. In a large skillet, heat the oil over medium heat. Add the onion, carrot, celery, and garlic and cook, stirring often, until the onion is softened, about 5 minutes. Stir in the potato and tomatoes. Transfer to a 3½-quart slow cooker and top with the browned short ribs and their juices. Pour in the beef broth.

3. Cover and slow-cook until the short ribs are tender, 7 to 8 hours on low (200°F). Using kitchen tongs, transfer the short ribs to a serving platter, and cover with foil to keep warm.

4. Skim the fat from the surface of the cooking liquid. Transfer the cooking liquid to a blender, add the horseradish and purée until smooth. Pour the sauce over the short ribs and serve immediately.

4 pounds beef short ribs

½ teaspoon salt

¼ teaspoon freshly ground black pepper

1 tablespoon vegetable oil

1 medium onion, chopped

1 medium carrot, cut into ½-inch-thick rounds

1 medium celery rib, cut into ½-inch-thick slices

2 garlic cloves, crushed

1 medium baking potato, peeled and chopped into ½-inch cubes

1 15-ounce can peeled Italian tomatoes, drained

¼ cup double-strength beef broth, canned or homemade

2 tablespoons prepared horseradish, or more to taste

Harvesttime Pork and Apple Stew

Pork and apples are a happy union and create a great stew with a gravy to enjoy on a chilly fall evening. I serve this with steamed baby carrots and Giant Potato Cake (page 233).

Makes 4 to 6 servings

1. In a large skillet, heat the oil over medium-high heat. Add the pork cubes, in batches without crowding, and cook, turning often, until browned on all sides, about 5 minutes. Transfer to a plate and season with the salt and pepper.

2. Add more oil to the skillet, if necessary, and heat over medium heat. Add the onions, carrots, and apples and cook, stirring often, until the onions are beginning to brown, about 6 minutes. Transfer to a 3½-quart slow cooker and top with the pork cubes and their juices.

3. Add the apple cider, vermouth, Calvados, thyme, allspice, and sage to the skillet. Bring to a simmer, scraping up the browned bits on the bottom of the pan with a wooden spoon. Pour into the slow cooker.

4. Cover and slow-cook until the pork is tender, 6 to 7 hours on low (200°F). Using a slotted spoon, transfer the meat to a serving bowl, and cover with foil to keep warm.

5. Skim off the fat from the surface of the cooking liquid. In a food processor or blender, purée the cooking liquid and solids until smooth. Pour the sauce over the meat, stir gently, and serve immediately.

2 tablespoons vegetable oil, plus more if needed

3 pounds boneless pork shoulder, cut into 2-inch cubes and well trimmed

½ teaspoon salt

¼ teaspoon freshly ground black pepper

2 medium onions, chopped

2 medium carrots, cut into ½-inch-thick rounds

2 medium Granny Smith apples, peeled, cored, and quartered

¾ cup freshly squeezed apple cider

¼ cup dry vermouth

2 tablespoons Calvados, applejack, or brandy

½ teaspoon dried thyme

¼ teaspoon ground allspice

¼ teaspoon rubbed sage

Pork, Port, and Chestnut Ragoût

Fresh chestnuts are one of the real joys of fall cooking, and they pair up admirably with pork. If fresh chestnuts are unavailable, you may be able to find vacuum-packed cooked chestnuts at your supermarket or specialty food store; they are an acceptable, though pricy, substitute.

Makes 4 to 6 servings

1. In a large skillet, heat the oil over medium-high heat. Add the pork, in batches without crowding, and cook, turning often, until browned on all sides, about 5 minutes. Transfer to a plate and season with the salt and pepper.

2. Add more oil to the skillet, if necessary, and heat over medium heat. Add the onion and cook, stirring often, until lightly browned, about 6 minutes. Transfer to a 3½-quart slow cooker, and stir in the baby carrots. Top with the pork and its juices. Add the beef broth, port, thyme, and bay leaf. Cover and slow-cook until the pork is tender, 5 to 6 hours on low (200°F). Add the chestnuts and cook until they are heated through, about 30 minutes longer.

3. Using a slotted spoon, transfer the pork, vegetables, and chestnuts to a serving bowl, and cover with foil to keep warm. Skim the fat from the surface of the cooking liquid.

4. In a medium saucepan, melt the butter over low heat. Add the flour and cook, whisking constantly, without browning, for 1

2 tablespoons vegetable oil, plus more if needed

2½ pounds boneless pork loin, cut into 2-inch pieces and well trimmed

1 teaspoon salt

¼ teaspoon freshly ground black pepper

1 medium onion, chopped

1 pound baby carrots, peeled

½ cup double-strength beef or chicken broth, canned or homemade

⅓ cup tawny or vintage port

½ teaspoon dried thyme

1 bay leaf

1 pound fresh chestnuts, roasted and peeled, or 1 16-ounce jar vacuum-packed chestnuts

2 tablespoons unsalted butter

2 tablespoons all-purpose flour

minute. Whisk in the cooking liquid and bring to a boil. Cook, whisking often, until the sauce has thickened and reduced to about 1¼ cups, 6 to 8 minutes. Pour the sauce over the pork ragout, mix gently, and serve immediately.

To roast and peel chestnuts, make a deep "X" in the flat side of each chestnut with a small sharp knife. Bake in a preheated 400°F oven until the outer peel is split and the chestnuts are tender, 25 to 35 minutes. While they are still warm, remove the tough outer peels and inner skins. To remove stubborn skins, reheat in the oven for 5 to 10 minutes more.

Pork and Sausage Cazuela

Pork, chorizo sausage, sweet peppers, and olives combine in this rich stew, with sherry adding an Iberian note to the sauce.

Makes 6 servings

1. In a medium bowl, combine the paprika, salt, and cayenne. Add the pork cubes and toss well to coat with the spice mixture.

2. Place the potatoes in the bottom of a 3½-quart slow cooker.

3. In a large skillet, heat the oil over medium-high heat. Add the pork cubes, in batches without crowding, and cook, turning often, until browned on all sides, about 5 minutes. Transfer to the slow cooker.

4. Add the onion and bell pepper to the skillet, adding more oil if necessary. Reduce the heat to medium and cook, stirring often, until softened, about 5 minutes. Add the garlic and cook, stirring often, for 1 minute. Add the water, tomato paste, rosemary, and bay leaves. Bring to a simmer, stirring to blend in the tomato paste and scraping up the browned bits on the bottom of the skillet. Pour into the slow cooker. Add the chicken broth and sherry and stir gently, but leave the potatoes in place. Cover and slow-cook until the pork is tender, 6 to 7 hours on low (200°F).

5. Meanwhile, in a medium skillet, cook the sausage over medium heat, stirring often, until browned, about 6 minutes.

6. Stir the cooked chorizo, the peas, and olives into the slow cooker. Cover and cook just until heated through, about 15 min-

1 tablespoon sweet Hungarian paprika

1 teaspoon salt

¼ teaspoon cayenne pepper

3 pounds boneless pork shoulder, well trimmed and cut into 2-inch pieces

3 medium boiling potatoes, scrubbed and cut into ½-inch-thick rounds

2 tablespoons olive oil, plus more if needed

1 large onion, chopped

1 large red bell pepper, seeded and chopped

3 garlic cloves, minced

½ cup water

2 tablespoons tomato paste

1½ teaspoons dried rosemary

2 bay leaves

1 cup double-strength chicken broth, canned or homemade

½ cup dry sherry

utes. Using a slotted spoon, transfer the meat and vegetables to a serving bowl, and cover with foil to keep warm. Skim the fat from the surface of the sauce.

7. In a medium saucepan over low heat, melt the butter. Add the flour and cook, whisking constantly, without browning, for 1 minute. Whisk in the cooking liquid and bring to a simmer. Cook, whisking often, until reduced to about 1½ cups, 6 to 8 minutes. Pour the sauce over the stew, mix gently, and serve immediately.

4 chorizo sausages or other spicy smoked sausages (about 2 ounces each), cut into ½-inch rounds

1 10-ounce package frozen petite peas, defrosted

½ cup pitted green Spanish olives, rinsed

2 tablespoons unsalted butter

2 tablespoons all-purpose flour

Chinese Country Ribs

These delectably moist ribs make plenty of sweet and sour sauce to serve over hot rice. Make Chinese Cabbage and Peanut Slaw (page 227) to serve alongside.

Makes 4 servings

1. In a 3½-quart slow cooker, combine the catsup, honey, vinegar, soy sauce, five-spice powder, onion, ginger, and garlic.

2. Position a broiler rack 6 inches from the source of heat and preheat the broiler. Broil the ribs, turning once, until browned, about 10 minutes. Transfer the ribs to the slow cooker. Stir to coat the ribs with the sauce.

3. Cover and slow-cook until the ribs are tender, 5 to 6 hours on low (200°F). Transfer the ribs to a platter and cover with aluminum foil to keep warm.

4. Skim the fat from the surface of the sauce. In a medium saucepan, bring the sauce to a simmer over medium heat. Cook until reduced to about 1 cup, 6 to 8 minutes. Stir in the cornstarch mixture, and cook just until thickened. Pour the sauce over the ribs and serve immediately with hot cooked rice.

Hill Country Ribs: *Broil the ribs as in Step 1 and place in a 3½-quart slow cooker. Add 1 cup prepared barbecue sauce and stir to coat the ribs with the sauce. Cover and slow-cook until the ribs are tender, 5 to 6 hours on low (200°F). To thicken the sauce, skim the fat from the surface, pour into a medium saucepan, and simmer until reduced to about 1 cup.*

½ cup catsup

2 tablespoons honey

2 tablespoons rice or white vinegar

2 tablespoons soy sauce

¼ teaspoon five-spice powder (optional)

1 small onion, finely chopped

2 teaspoons minced fresh ginger

1 garlic clove, minced

1 teaspoon cornstarch dissolved in 1 tablespoon cold water

Hot cooked rice

4 pounds country ribs, cut into individual ribs

Greek Veal and Baby Onion Stifado

Stifado is a popular Greek country stew. To be a true *stifado,* the dish must contain equal amounts of onions and meat and be seasoned with a splash of vinegar. (The Greeks cook with vinegar more than with wine, as they prefer their wine to be flavored with resin—not your best stew seasoning.) The slow cooker melds the veal and onion flavors in an incomparable fashion.

Makes 4 to 6 servings

1. In a large skillet, heat the oil over medium-high heat. Add the veal, in batches without crowding, and cook, turning often, until browned. Transfer to a 3 ½-quart slow cooker, season with the salt and pepper, and stir well.

2. Add the peeled boiling onions to the skillet, adding more oil if necessary. Reduce the heat to medium and cook, turning often, until lightly browned on all sides, about 5 minutes. Stir into the slow cooker. Add the tomatoes with their purée, the vinegar, allspice, oregano, cumin, and cinnamon stick, stirring to break up the tomatoes with the side of a spoon.

3. Cover and slow-cook until the veal is tender, 6 to 7 hours on low (200°F). Skim the fat from the surface of the stew and serve directly from the slow cooker.

2 tablespoons olive oil, plus more if needed

2 pounds boneless veal shoulder, cut into 2-inch pieces

½ teaspoon salt

¼ teaspoon freshly ground black pepper

2 pounds small boiling onions, peeled (see page 97)

1 28-ounce can peeled tomatoes in thick tomato purée

¼ cup red wine vinegar

½ teaspoon ground allspice

½ teaspoon dried oregano

¼ teaspoon ground cumin

1 3-inch cinnamon stick

Indonesian Veal Stew with Coconut and Peanuts

This stew is equally tasty made with beef, pork, or lamb. I've even made it with chicken (reducing the cooking time to about five and a half hours).

Makes 4 to 6 servings

1. In a medium bowl, combine the curry powder, salt, ginger, cumin, and cayenne. Set aside.

2. In a large skillet, heat the oil over medium-high heat. Add the veal, in batches without crowding, and cook, turning often, until lightly browned on all sides. Transfer to a bowl, add the soy sauce, and toss well.

3. Add the onion and chile pepper to the skillet, adding more oil if necessary. Reduce the heat to medium and cook, stirring often, until softened, about 5 minutes. Return the veal to the skillet, and add the garlic. Sprinkle with the spice mixture and stir for 1 minute; do not let the spices scorch. Transfer to a 3½-quart slow cooker, and stir in the coconut.

4. Cover and slow-cook until the veal is tender, 6 to 7 hours on low (200°F). Stir in the peanuts and yogurt, and serve immediately.

While unsweetened coconut is available in some health food stores, the sweetened variety is easier to find, but it must be rinsed of its sugar coating to use in a savory dish. To remove this coating, place the coconut in a wire strainer, rinse well under hot water, and then pat the coconut dry with paper towels.

2 teaspoons curry powder

1 teaspoon salt

1 teaspoon ground ginger

½ teaspoon ground cumin

⅛ teaspoon cayenne pepper

2 tablespoons vegetable oil, plus more if needed

2½ pounds boneless veal shoulder, well trimmed and cut into 2-inch pieces

2 tablespoons soy sauce

1 medium onion, chopped

1 fresh hot green chile pepper (such as jalapeño), seeded and minced

2 garlic cloves, minced

1 cup shredded unsweetened or sweetened coconut flakes, rinsed

½ cup unsalted peanuts

½ cup plain low-fat yogurt

Osso Buco

Osso buco, the classic Italian veal shank dish, is excellent with Saffron Herbed Rice (page 232), a stand-in for the traditional side dish of risotto.

Makes 4 servings

1. In a large skillet, heat the oil over medium-high heat. Add the veal shanks, in batches without crowding, and cook, turning once, until browned, about 5 minutes. Transfer to a plate and season with the salt and pepper.

2. Add the onion, carrot, and celery to the skillet, and add more oil if necessary. Reduce the heat to medium and cook, stirring often, until the onion is softened, about 5 minutes. Add half the garlic and cook, stirring often, for 1 minute. Add the wine, broth, and marjoram and bring to a boil, stirring up the browned bits on the bottom of the skillet. Remove from the heat and stir in the tomatoes, breaking them up with a spoon. Transfer to a 3½-quart slow cooker, and stack the veal shanks with their juices on top.

3. Cover and cook until the veal is tender, 7 to 8 hours on low (200°F). Using a slotted spoon, transfer the veal shanks to a platter and cover with foil to keep warm.

4. Skim the fat from the surface of the cooking liquid and pour into a medium saucepan. Bring to a boil and cook until slightly thickened, about 5 minutes.

5. Meanwhile, in a small bowl, combine the lemon zest, parsley, and remaining garlic. Pour the sauce over the veal shanks, sprinkle with the lemon mixture, and serve immediately.

2 tablespoons olive oil, plus more if needed

4 pounds veal shanks, sawed crosswise into 1½-inch-thick pieces (have the butcher do this)

½ teaspoon salt

¼ teaspoon freshly ground black pepper

1 medium onion, finely chopped

1 medium carrot, finely chopped

1 medium celery rib, finely chopped

2 garlic cloves, minced, divided

½ cup dry white wine

½ cup double-strength chicken broth, canned or homemade

¾ teaspoon dried marjoram

1 15-ounce can peeled Italian tomatoes, drained

Grated zest of 1 lemon

2 tablespoons chopped fresh parsley

Lamb, Mushroom, and Barley Pilaf

I am always looking for opportunities to cook with barley. With its unique chewy texture, barley usually plays a supporting role, dotting soups and stews. Here it's elevated to star status, soaking up all of the juices in a lamb and mushroom ragoût to form a robust pilaf.

Makes 4 to 6 servings

1. In a large skillet, heat the oil over medium-high heat. Add the lamb, in batches without crowding, and cook, turning often, until browned on all sides. Transfer to a 3½-quart slow cooker, season with the salt and pepper, and stir well.

2. Add the onion and mushrooms to the skillet, adding more oil if necessary. Reduce the heat to medium and cook, stirring often, until the mushrooms have given up their liquid and are beginning to brown, about 7 minutes. Transfer to the slow cooker.

3. Add the beef broth, wine, and thyme to the skillet and bring to a boil, stirring up the browned bits on the bottom of the pan. Pour into the slow cooker and mix well.

4. Cover and slow-cook until the lamb is almost tender, 5 to 6 hours on low (200°F). Skim the fat from the surface of the cooking liquid.

5. Turn the heat to high (300°F) and stir in the barley. Cover and cook until the barley and lamb are tender, about 1 hour. Sprinkle with the parsley and serve immediately.

2 tablespoons olive oil, plus more if needed

2½ pounds boneless lamb shoulder, cut into 2-inch pieces and well trimmed

1 teaspoon salt

¼ teaspoon freshly ground black pepper

1 large onion, chopped

10 ounces fresh mushrooms, sliced

¾ cup double-strength beef broth, canned or homemade

¼ cup dry white wine or dry vermouth

1 teaspoon dried thyme

½ cup barley

2 tablespoons chopped fresh parsley

Shepherd's Stew

Lamb, potatoes, and peas combine to make a flavorful rendition of Irish stew.

Makes 4 to 6 servings

1. Place the potatoes in the bottom of a 3½-quart slow cooker.

2. In a large skillet, heat the oil over medium-high heat. Add the lamb, in batches without crowding, and cook, turning often, until browned, about 5 minutes. Transfer the lamb to the slow cooker, and season with the salt and pepper.

3. Add more oil to the skillet, if necessary, and heat over medium heat. Add the onion and cook, stirring often, until softened, about 5 minutes. Add the garlic and cook, stirring often, for 1 minute. Add the beef broth, parsley, tomato paste, and Worcestershire sauce, and stir to scrape up the browned bits on the bottom of the skillet. Transfer to the slow cooker, cover, and slow-cook until the lamb is tender, 6 to 7 hours on low (200°F).

4. Meanwhile, in a small bowl, mash the butter with the flour to form a smooth paste.

5. Skim the fat from the surface of the cooking liquid. Whisk about ⅓ cup of the cooking liquid into the butter mixture until smooth, then stir into the stew. Stir in the peas. Increase the heat to high (300°F), and cook until the sauce is thickened, about 15 minutes. Serve directly from the slow cooker.

3 medium potatoes, scrubbed and cut into ½-inch-thick rounds

2 tablespoons vegetable oil, plus more if needed

3 pounds boneless lamb shoulder, well trimmed and cut into 2-inch pieces

1 teaspoon salt

¼ teaspoon freshly ground black pepper

1 large onion, chopped

2 garlic cloves, minced

½ cup double-strength beef broth

2 tablespoons chopped fresh parsley

1 tablespoon tomato paste

1 tablespoon Worcestershire sauce

2 tablespoons unsalted butter, softened

2 tablespoons all-purpose flour

1 cup frozen peas, defrosted

Lamb in Chile Rojo Sauce

This chili/stew, with an incendiary brick-red sauce, comes from the kitchens of New Mexico. It's made with lots of local dried chiles, which now can be found in the produce departments of many supermarkets nationwide. Even though this dish is plenty hot, I think you'll find it creates the kind of warmth that is a pleasant glow, and not a raging blaze. I like to make this with bone-in lamb neck chunks, as the flavor from the bones seems to temper the chiles' heat, but you can use boneless lamb shoulder if you prefer.

Makes 4 servings

3 ounces dried New Mexican chiles

3 cups boiling water

1 medium onion, chopped

6 garlic cloves, minced

1/4 cup tomato paste

1 1/2 teaspoons dried marjoram

1 teaspoon salt

1/4 teaspoon freshly ground black pepper

2 tablespoons olive oil

4 pounds bone-in lamb neck or 2 pounds boneless lamb shoulder, cut into 2-inch cubes and well trimmed

1 cup double-strength beef broth, canned or homemade

1. Split open the chiles under cold running water (protecting your hands with rubber gloves, if desired), and rinse out the seeds; discard the stems. In a medium bowl, combine the chiles with the boiling water. Cover and let soak until the chiles are softened, about 1 hour. (The chiles can be soaked overnight at room temperature if desired.) Drain the chiles, reserving 1 cup of the soaking liquid.

2. In a food processor, combine the softened chiles, the onion, garlic, tomato paste, marjoram, salt, and pepper. With the machine running, gradually pour in the reserved soaking liquid, and process until smooth. Transfer the chile sauce to a 3 1/2-quart slow cooker.

3. In a large skillet, heat the oil over medium-high heat. Add the lamb, in batches without crowding, and cook, turning often, until browned on all sides. Transfer to the slow cooker. Pour the beef broth into the skillet and bring to a boil, scraping up the browned bits on the bottom of the skillet. Stir into the slow cooker. Cover and slow-cook until the meat is tender, 7 to 8 hours on low (200°F).

4. Using a slotted spoon, transfer the meat to a deep serving bowl. Skim the fat off the surface of the sauce, pour the sauce over the meat, and serve. (This stew is best made one day ahead, so the flavors can mellow. Let the stew cool to room temperature, then cover and refrigerate. To serve, scrape the hardened fat off the surface of the stew, then reheat gently.)

New Mexican dried chile peppers are relatively mild; do not substitute other chile varieties unless you are willing to experiment with your heat tolerance level. They are available by mail order from The Chile Shop, 109 East Water Street, Santa Fe, New Mexico 87501; (505) 983-6080.

Lamb Vindaloo

This is a must-try for Indian food fanatics. Chunks of lamb are marinated in an exotic vinegar and spice paste, then slow-cooked. The resulting mixture is fried in a large pot to evaporate the juices and sear the seasonings onto the meat.

Makes 4 to 6 servings

1.   In a food processor, process the onion, ginger, and garlic until finely chopped. Add the vinegar, coriander, cumin, turmeric, salt, and cayenne pepper and process until the mixture forms a smooth paste. Transfer the paste to a 3½-quart slow-cooker crockery insert. Add the lamb and toss to coat well with the paste. Cover with plastic wrap and refrigerate at least 4 hours, or overnight.

2.   Place the crockery insert in the slow cooker and stir in the water. Cover, and slow-cook until the lamb is tender, 6 to 7 hours on low (200°F).

3.   Transfer the lamb and cooking juices to a large saucepan. Cook over medium-high heat, stirring often, until all the liquid has evaporated and the lamb is sizzling, about 20 minutes. Reduce the heat to low and continue cooking, stirring often, until the spice coating turns light brown, about 5 additional minutes. Serve immediately.

1 medium onion, quartered

1 1-inch piece fresh ginger, peeled

2 garlic cloves, crushed

⅓ cup red wine vinegar

1 tablespoon ground coriander

1 tablespoon ground cumin

1 tablespoon turmeric

1 teaspoon salt

¼ teaspoon cayenne pepper

3 pounds boneless lamb shoulder, cut into 2-inch pieces and well trimmed

1 cup water

Lamb Shanks in Garlic Sauce

I've always been a lamb fan, particularly of the succulent shanks. Here lamb is paired with one of its best allies, garlic. The garlic's aggressiveness is tamed by long cooking, so don't be alarmed at using a whole head.

Makes 4 servings

1. In a small saucepan of boiling water, blanch the garlic cloves for 1 minute. Drain, rinse under cold running water, and drain again. Peel the garlic cloves and place in a 3 ½-quart slow cooker.

2. Position a broiler rack about 6 inches from the source of heat and preheat the broiler. Season the lamb shanks with the salt and pepper. Broil the lamb shanks, turning once, until browned, about 15 minutes. Pack the lamb shanks into the slow cooker and sprinkle with the rosemary. Pour in the wine and broth.

3. Cover and cook until the lamb is tender, 6 to 7 hours on low (200°F). Transfer the lamb shanks to a platter and cover with foil to keep warm.

4. Skim the fat from the surface of the sauce. Place a wire strainer over a medium saucepan, and press the sauce through the strainer; be sure to scrape the garlic from the underside of the strainer into the pan. Bring to a boil over high heat and cook until reduced to about ⅔ cup, 8 to 10 minutes. Pour the sauce over the lamb shanks, sprinkle with the parsley, and serve immediately.

1 head garlic, separated into unpeeled cloves

4 lamb shanks (about 1¼ pounds each) sawed crosswise into 2-inch pieces (have the butcher do this)

¼ teaspoon salt

¼ teaspoon freshly ground black pepper

1 teaspoon dried rosemary

¼ cup dry white wine

¼ cup double-strength beef broth, canned or homemade

2 tablespoons chopped fresh parsley or mint

Sauerkraut and Sausage Casserole Alsace

Makes 4 to 6 servings

1. In a medium skillet, cook the bacon over medium heat, stirring often, until browned and crisp, about 5 minutes. Using a slotted spoon transfer the bacon to paper towels to drain. Drain off all but 2 tablespoons of fat from the skillet.

2. Add the onion and carrot to the skillet and cook, stirring often, until the onion is softened, about 5 minutes. Add the garlic and cook, stirring often, for 1 minute. Stir in the sauerkraut, cooked bacon, the thyme, caraway seeds, pepper, and bay leaf.

3. Place the potatoes in a 3½-quart slow cooker. Add the sauerkraut mixture, and pour in the wine, chicken broth, and gin. Cover and slow-cook until the potatoes are tender, 6 to 7 hours on low (200°F).

4. Make 3 diagonal slashes about 1 inch long and ⅛ inch deep in each sausage, and bury the sausages and apples in the sauerkraut. Increase the heat to high (300°F), uncover, and continue slow-cooking until the excess liquid has evaporated and the sausages are heated through, about 1 hour.

5. Remove the bay leaf and serve the casserole with the mustard passed on the side.

Fresh sauerkraut is found in plastic bags or glass jars in the refrigerated section of supermarkets. Avoid canned sauerkraut if you can.

4 slices bacon, cut into 1-inch-wide pieces

1 medium onion, chopped

1 medium carrot, chopped

1 garlic clove, minced

2 pounds fresh sauerkraut, rinsed and squeezed to remove excess moisture

1 teaspoon dried thyme

1 teaspoon caraway seeds

¼ teaspoon black pepper

1 bay leaf

3 medium boiling potatoes, scrubbed, unpeeled, and cut into ½-inch-thick rounds

½ cup dry white wine or dry vermouth

¼ cup double-strength chicken broth, canned or homemade

2 tablespoons gin (optional)

8 smoked sausages, such as knockwurst, bratwurst, or kielbasa (about 1½ pounds)

2 medium Granny Smith apples, peeled, cored, and coarsely chopped

Prepared mustard

Ravioli Casserole

Casseroles are the ultimate comfort food. Here's one of my "Top Ten," with the ingredients for my favorite raviolis, but mixed up and cooked the slow cooker way.

Makes 4 to 6 servings

1. In a large skillet over medium-high heat, cook the ground beef, onion, and garlic, stirring often to break up lumps, until the meat loses its pink color, about 5 minutes. Tilt the pan to drain off excess fat, then transfer the beef mixture to a 3½-quart slow cooker.

2. Add the tomatoes with their purée, the tomato sauce, Italian seasoning, and pepper, stirring to break up the tomatoes with the side of a spoon. Cover and slow-cook for 7 to 8 hours on low (200°F).

3. Skim the fat from the surface of meat sauce. Stir in the cooked pasta, spinach, and ricotta and Parmesan cheeses, and slow-cook for 5 minutes. Serve the casserole directly from the slow cooker.

1½ pounds lean ground beef

1 medium onion, chopped

2 garlic cloves, minced

1 28-ounce can peeled tomatoes in thick tomato purée

1 15-ounce can tomato sauce

2 teaspoons Italian herb seasoning

¼ teaspoon freshly ground black pepper

1 pound bow-tie pasta or fettuccine, freshly cooked

1 10-ounce package frozen chopped spinach, defrosted and squeezed to remove excess moisture

2 cups ricotta cheese

½ cup freshly grated imported Parmesan cheese

Spaghetti in Herbed Tomato Sauce with Parmesan Meatballs

There are few dishes more satisfying or fun to eat than spaghetti and meatballs. The secret to tender meatballs, whether using a slow-cooker or not, is to skip the usual preliminary browning in oil. They will hold their shape beautifully if simply dropped into the tomato sauce and poached. This is one of my favorite Sunday suppers—I can spend the whole afternoon running errands while the slow cooker is doing all the work. And the tomato sauce won't scorch, either!

Makes 4 to 6 servings

1. *For the sauce:* In a medium skillet, heat the oil over medium heat. Add the onion and cook until softened, about 5 minutes. Add the garlic and stir for 1 minute. Transfer to a 3½-quart slow cooker. Stir in the tomatoes, tomato paste, red wine, basil, oregano, rosemary, and hot red pepper.

2. *For the meatballs:* In a large bowl, combine the bread crumbs and milk; let stand for 5 minutes.

3. Add the ground beef, onion, garlic, egg, Parmesan cheese, parsley, salt, and pepper and mix just until blended. Scoop up a heaping tablespoon of the meat mixture, roll into a meatball, and drop into the tomato sauce. Repeat with the remaining meat mixture to make 12 meatballs in all. Cover and cook until the meatballs are cooked through, 5 to 6 hours on low (200°F).

HERBED TOMATO SAUCE

1 tablespoon olive oil

1 medium onion, chopped

1 garlic clove, minced

3 15-ounce cans peeled Italian tomatoes, drained and chopped

1 6-ounce can tomato paste

¼ cup dry red wine

1 teaspoon dried basil

1 teaspoon dried oregano

1 teaspoon dried rosemary

¼ teaspoon crushed hot red pepper

PARMESAN MEATBALLS

¾ cup fresh bread crumbs

¼ cup milk

1 pound lean ground beef

1 medium onion, finely chopped

1 garlic clove, minced

1 large egg, lightly beaten

4. Place the cooked spaghetti in a warmed serving bowl. With a slotted spoon, transfer the meatballs to the bowl of spaghetti. Skim the fat from the surface of the sauce. Pour the sauce over the spaghetti, mix well, and serve immediately, passing a bowl of grated cheese on the side.

3 tablespoons freshly grated imported Parmesan cheese

2 tablespoons chopped fresh parsley

1 teaspoon salt

1/4 teaspoon freshly ground black pepper

1 pound spaghetti, freshly cooked

Freshly grated imported Parmesan cheese

Slow-Cooked Meat Loaf

I have cooked scores of meat loaves in my day, but this is the tried-and-true slow-cooked version I make most often. I like my meat loaf with catsup both inside and outside, and with beef, veal, and pork together. The slow cooker does a very creditable job with meat loaf. And, since the loaf cooks on a rack, the fat drips out and collects underneath the loaf. But you'll need some help getting the loaf in and out of the crockery insert; a simple "cradle" of aluminum foil strips does the job easily.

Makes 4 servings

⅔ cup dried bread crumbs

⅓ cup plus 2 tablespoons catsup, divided

1 small onion, finely chopped

1 large egg

1 tablespoon Worcestershire sauce

1 teaspoon salt

¼ teaspoon freshly ground black pepper

1 pound lean ground beef

½ pound ground pork

½ pound ground veal

1. In a large bowl, mix the oats, the ⅓ cup catsup, the onion, egg, Worcestershire sauce, salt, and pepper. Add the ground beef, pork, and veal and mix well. Shape into a 7-inch round loaf.

2. Place a collapsible vegetable steamer or a slow cooker meat rack in the bottom of a 3½-quart slow cooker. Tear off two 24-inch-long pieces of aluminum foil. Fold each piece lengthwise in half, and then in half again, making two strips about 3 inches wide. Place one strip on top of the other, intersecting at their centers, to form a cross. Place the meat loaf in the center of the cross. Bring the ends of the cross up to meet above the loaf, forming a handle. Lift the loaf up by the foil handle and place on the steamer or meat rack. Fold the foil handle strips over the top of the loaf.

3. Cover and cook until the meat loaf is cooked through and a meat thermometer inserted in the center of the loaf reads 165 degrees, 6 to 7 hours on low (200°F). About 15 minutes before the meat loaf is done, unfold the foil strips and let them hang over the edges of the slow cooker. Spread the top of the meat loaf with the remaining 2 tablespoons catsup. Replace the top firmly, increase the heat to high (300°F), and cook until the catsup is set, about 15 minutes.

4.   To remove the meat loaf from the slow cooker, bring the foil strips up to form a handle again, lift and transfer the loaf to a plate. Slide the foil strips out from the loaf before serving.

Pot Roasts

Pot roasts, large cuts of meat braised with savory vegetables in a succulent sauce, are ideal for supper. I often prepare a pot roast on Sunday morning, allowing me to spend the remainder of the day as I like. As dinner approaches, I can continue the relaxed mood, since my main course is ready and waiting.

For beef pot roasts, such as The Pot Roast, I prefer bottom round, because it turns out juicy and easy to slice. Chuck roast, featured in Belgian Beer and Onion Pot Roast, must be well trimmed, and then browned to remove excess fat. Sweet and Sour Beef Brisket shows how beautifully brisket braises, but choose the thinner, leaner first cut. Well-trimmed pork picnic roast makes an admirable pot roast, as Joy's Mexican Pot Roast illustrates, but be sure to skim the cooking liquid well. Boneless pork roast loin is a fine choice, but note that the cooking time is five to six hours, less than is allowed for most of the other pot roasts.

No matter what kind of pot roast you prepare, keep the size of the crockery insert in mind. Large pieces of meat can be cut into pieces and stacked to fit into the slow cooker. As with stews, be sure the meat is well trimmed so excess fat won't raise the temperature of the cooking liquid and boil your pot roast.

The Pot Roast

Makes 4 to 6 servings

1. In a large skillet, heat the oil over medium-high heat. Add the roast and cook, turning often, until browned on all sides, about 10 minutes. Transfer the roast to a plate and season with ½ teaspoon of the salt and ¼ teaspoon of the pepper.

2. Add more oil to the skillet, if necessary, and heat over medium heat. Add the onions, carrots, and potatoes and cook over medium heat, stirring often, until the onions are softened, about 5 minutes. Transfer the vegetables to a 3½-quart slow cooker. Add the bay leaves, and season with the remaining ½ teaspoon salt and ¼ teaspoon pepper. Place the roast on top of the vegetables.

3. Add the water to the skillet and bring to a boil, scraping up the browned bits on the bottom of the pan with a wooden spoon. Pour into the slow cooker.

4. Cover and slow-cook until the roast is very tender, 8 to 10 hours on low (200°F). Using a slotted spoon, transfer the roast and the vegetables to a platter and cover with foil to keep warm. Skim the fat from the surface of the cooking liquid.

5. In a saucepan, melt the butter over very low heat. Add the flour and let bubble, stirring constantly, until lightly browned, about 1 minute. Whisk in the cooking liquid and bring to a simmer. Cook, whisking often, until thickened and reduced to about 1 cup, about 5 minutes.

6. Using a sharp, thin knife, slice the roast crosswise across the grain. Serve with the vegetables and gravy.

2 tablespoons vegetable oil, plus more if needed

1 3½ pound-beef bottom round roast, well trimmed and tied

1 teaspoon salt, divided

½ teaspoon freshly ground black pepper, divided

2 medium onions, sliced

2 medium carrots, cut into ½-inch-thick rounds

4 medium boiling potatoes, cut into ½-inch-thick rounds

2 bay leaves

½ cup water

1 tablespoon unsalted butter

1 tablespoon all-purpose flour

Belgian Beer and Onion Pot Roast

The flavors for this pot roast are based on the Belgian stew called a *carbonnade,* in which the sweetness of caramelized onions is tempered by the slight bitterness of beer. The gravy gets zip from mustard and vinegar. Serve the pot roast with parslied new potatoes boiled in their skins, and plenty of cold beer.

Makes 4 to 5 servings

1. Cut the chuck roast crosswise into 2 or 3 large pieces to fit into a 3½-quart slow cooker.

2. In a large skillet, heat the oil over medium-high heat. Add the beef and cook, turning once, until browned, about 5 minutes. Transfer to a plate, season with the salt and pepper, and set aside.

3. Add the butter to the skillet and melt over medium heat. Add the onions and cook, stirring often, until lightly browned, about 7 minutes. Add the garlic and cook, stirring often, for 1 minute. Remove from the heat and stir in the beef broth, beer, brown sugar, mustard, and vinegar. Transfer to the slow cooker. Stack the chuck roast pieces on top of the onions.

4. Cover and cook until the meat is very tender, 7 to 8 hours on low (200°F). With a slotted spoon, transfer the pot roast and the onions to a platter and cover with foil to keep warm.

5. Skim the fat from the surface of the cooking liquid. In a medium saucepan, bring the cooking liquid to a simmer over medium heat. Stir in the cornstarch mixture and cook just until thickened. Pour the sauce over the pot roast and serve immediately.

1 2½-pound beef chuck roast, well trimmed

1 tablespoon vegetable oil

½ teaspoon salt

¼ teaspoon freshly ground black pepper

2 tablespoons unsalted butter

4 medium onions, sliced

2 garlic cloves, minced

½ cup double-strength beef broth, canned or homemade

½ cup lager beer

1 tablespoon light brown sugar

1 tablespoon Dijon mustard

1 tablespoon cider vinegar

2 teaspoons cornstarch dissolved in 1 tablespoon cold water

Carrot-Studded Pot Roast

When sliced, this pot roast reveals a striking decoration of carrot strips woven through the meat. Serve it with lots of hot pasta to soak up the cooking juices.

Makes 4 to 6 servings

1. Peel the carrots and cut each one into four 6-inch-long sticks about ¼ inch wide. Coarsely chop the carrot trimmings and reserve.

2. Using a long, thin knife, poke 8 evenly spaced holes all the way through the roast, beginning at the flat "face" and following the grain of the meat. Insert the carrot sticks into the holes. Using the tip of the knife, make 8 shallow incisions all over the meat, and insert the garlic slivers into them.

3. In a large skillet, heat the oil over medium-high heat. Add the roast and brown on all sides, about 10 minutes. Transfer the roast to a plate and season with the salt and pepper.

4. Add more oil to the skillet, if necessary, and heat over medium heat. Add the onion, celery, and reserved carrot trimmings and cook, stirring often, until the onion is softened, about 5 minutes. Stir in the tomatoes, red wine, Italian herbs, and bay leaf, and bring to a boil, stirring to break up the tomatoes with the side of a spoon.

5. Pour the tomato mixture into a 3½-quart slow cooker. Add the roast and its juices, cover, and slow-cook until the roast is tender, 8 to 10 hours on low (200°F).

2 medium carrots

1 3-pound beef bottom round roast

2 garlic cloves, 1 cut into 8 slivers and 1 minced

2 tablespoons olive oil, plus more if needed

½ teaspoon salt

¼ teaspoon freshly ground black pepper

1 medium onion, chopped

1 celery rib, chopped

1 15-ounce can peeled Italian tomatoes, drained

1 cup dry red wine, such as Zinfandel

1 teaspoon Italian herb seasoning

1 bay leaf

6 .   Transfer the roast to a platter and cover with foil to keep warm. Skim off any fat from the surface of the cooking liquid. In a medium saucepan, bring the cooking liquid to a boil over high heat and cook until the sauce has reduced to about 1¾ cups, 6 to 8 minutes.

7 .   Slice the roast across the grain into ½-inch-thick slices. Arrange the slices, overlapping, on the serving platter. Pour the sauce over the slices and let stand, covered, for 5 minutes before serving.

Joy's Mexican Pot Roast

Joy Dawson is the cooking school administrator of Buehler's Markets in Ohio. Her slow-cooking classes are always packed. She often teaches this pork roast, that while *magnifico* on its own, really shines when used in South of the Border Burritos (see page 129).

Makes 4 to 6 servings

1. In a large skillet, heat the oil over medium heat. Add the onions, carrots, and chiles. Cook, stirring often, until softened, about 5 minutes. Add the garlic and cook, stirring often, for 1 minute. Transfer to a 5-quart slow cooker, and place a collapsible vegetable steamer or a slow-cooker meat rack on top of the vegetables.

2. In a small bowl, combine the salt, oregano, cumin, coriander, and pepper.

3. Rub the seasonings into the pork roast. Place the pork roast on the steamer or meat rack, and pour in the chicken broth and water.

4. Cover and slow-cook until the pork is very tender, 7 to 8 hours on low (200°F). Using a slotted spoon, transfer the pork and vegetables to a serving platter and cover with foil to keep warm.

5. Skim the fat from the surface of the cooking liquid. In a medium saucepan over medium-high heat, bring the cooking liquid to a boil. Cook until reduced to about 1 cup. Pour into a sauceboat. Slice the pork roast and pour about ½ cup of the sauce over the slices. Serve with the vegetables and the remaining sauce passed on the side.

1 tablespoon olive oil

2 medium onions, sliced

2 medium carrots, cut into ½-inch rounds

2 fresh hot green chile peppers (such as jalapeño), seeded and minced, or 1 4-ounce can chopped chiles, drained and rinsed

2 garlic cloves, minced

2 teaspoons salt

½ teaspoon dried oregano

½ teaspoon ground cumin

½ teaspoon ground coriander

¼ teaspoon freshly ground black pepper

1 4½-pound bone-in pork shoulder roast (picnic), well trimmed

½ cup double-strength chicken broth, canned or homemade

½ cup water

South of the Border Burritos: *Heat 8 large flour tortillas. Heat two 16-ounce cans refried beans. Using two forks, shred the Mexican Pot Roast. For each burrito, spread a tortilla with about ½ cup of the warm beans. Top with about 1 cup of the shredded pork, with the cooked vegetables from the roast. Add your favorite salsa. Fold over the sides, and roll up into a thick cylinder. Repeat with the remaining ingredients. Makes 8 burritos.*

In order to accommodate a 4½-pound pork roast, this recipe uses a 5-quart slow cooker. For a 3½-quart slow cooker, use a 3-pound roast, and halve the amounts of all the ingredients except the oil. You may have to buy a whole pork roast (they run 6 to 8 pounds), and have the butcher cut off a 3-pound portion. Freeze the remainder to roast later, or cut into 2-inch chunks for a stew (removing the skin, fat, and bones).

Pot-au-Feu

My Parisian friend, Bruno, rhapsodizes about pot-au-feu, braised beef with vegetables, the same way an American might salivate over a hot fudge sundae. In France, this hearty dish is served as a complete meal, with the tasty broth served as a soup course, followed by the braised meat and vegetables. Bruno insists that a gelatinous cut of meat, such as the calf's foot used here, be part of the cooking liquid to give body to the broth. His other admonition ("And never let it boil!") is beautifully handled by the slow cooker.

Makes 4 to 6 servings

1.   In a medium saucepan of boiling water, cook half of the calf's foot pieces (see Note) or all of the veal bones for 5 minutes; drain well.

2.   In a 3½-quart slow cooker, layer the vegetables in the following order: celery root, carrots, onions, and celery. Add the blanched calf's foot or veal bones. Sprinkle with the parsley and thyme and add the bay leaf. Season the roast with the salt and pepper and place on top of the vegetables. Pour in the beef broth and water.

3.   Cover and slow-cook until the meat is tender, 8 to 9 hours on low (200°F). Using a slotted spoon, transfer the meat and vegetables to a platter, and cover with foil to keep warm.

4.   Skim the fat off the surface of the cooking liquid. Ladle the broth into bowls and serve as a first course. For the main course, slice the roast and serve with the vegetables, mustard, and pickles.

1 calf's foot, sawed into pieces (have your butcher do this), or 1 pound veal bones

1 medium knob celery root (celeriac), pared and cut into ½-inch cubes

2 medium carrots, cut into ½-inch-thick rounds

2 medium onions, halved

2 medium celery ribs, cut into ½-inch-thick pieces

2 tablespoons chopped fresh parsley

½ teaspoon dried thyme

1 bay leaf

1 3-pound boneless beef rump or bottom round roast, well trimmed

½ teaspoon salt

¼ teaspoon freshly ground black pepper

2⅔ cups double-strength beef broth, homemade or canned

3 cups water

Dijon mustard and cornichons

130

Variation: *Stir 1 cup hot cooked rice or tiny pasta shapes (such as orzo) into the broth just before serving.*

Note: You need only half a calf's foot to give enough body to the broth. Wrap the remainder in foil and freeze for up to 2 months for another use. Add to any stew to give flavor and body to the sauce.

Sweet and Sour Beef Brisket

This is a tender and flavorful roast smothered with a chunky onion-carrot-raisin sauce. "First-cut brisket" refers to the thinner, leanest portion (the first portion the butcher prepares when he divides up the whole brisket).

Makes 4 to 6 servings

1. In a 3½-quart slow cooker, mix the orange and lemon juices, brown sugar, and tomato paste. Stir in the onions, carrots, and raisins.
2. Cut the brisket crosswise into 2 or 3 large pieces to fit into the slow cooker and season with the salt and pepper. Stack the brisket pieces on top of the vegetables.
3. Cover and cook until the meat is tender, 8 to 9 hours on low (200°F). Using a slotted spoon, transfer the brisket and the onions, carrots, and raisins to a platter, and cover with foil to keep warm.
4. Skim the fat from the surface of the cooking liquid. In a medium saucepan, bring the cooking liquid to a simmer over medium heat. Stir in the cornstarch mixture and cook just until thickened. Pour the sauce over the brisket and serve immediately.

½ cup orange juice

2 tablespoons lemon juice

2 tablespoons light brown sugar

1 tablespoon tomato paste

2 medium onions, thinly sliced

2 medium carrots, cut into ½-inch rounds

½ cup dark raisins

1 3-pound first-cut beef brisket

¼ teaspoon salt

¼ teaspoon freshly ground black pepper

1 tablespoon cornstarch dissolved in 2 tablespoons cold water

Erna's Sauerbraten

My friend Erna Zahn knows my soft spot for German foods, especially her sauerbraten. Erna's sauerbraten gravy includes the traditional thickening of gingersnap crumbs, along with a very un-German twist—balsamic vinegar! The roast takes a long steeping in a spiced vinegar and wine marinade, as well as long, slow cooking, so plan ahead. Please serve your sauerbraten with Sweet and Sour Red Cabbage (slow-cooked a day ahead and reheated) and Giant Potato Cake (pages 175 and 233).

Makes 4 to 6 servings

1. *For the marinade:* In a medium saucepan, combine all the marinade ingredients and bring to a simmer over medium heat. Cook for 5 minutes. Pour into a large nonreactive bowl and cool to room temperature.

2. Add the beef to the marinade, cover, and refrigerate for 2, or preferably 3, days. Turn the beef in the marinade as often as you can remember.

3. Remove the beef from the marinade and pat dry with paper towels. Strain the marinade into a bowl, and discard the solids. Reserve 1 cup of the marinade, and discard the rest.

4. In a large skillet, heat the oil over medium-high heat. Add the beef and cook, turning often, until browned on all sides, about 10 minutes. Transfer to a plate and season with the salt and pepper.

5. Add more oil to the skillet, if needed, and heat over medium heat. Add the onion, carrot, and celery and cook, stirring often,

MARINADE

1 cup dry red wine, such as Zinfandel

¾ cup red wine vinegar

¾ cup water

2 medium onions, sliced

1 medium carrot, chopped

1 medium celery rib, chopped

½ teaspoon whole allspice berries

¼ teaspoon whole cloves

¼ teaspoon black peppercorns

2 bay leaves

1 3½-pound beef bottom round roast, well trimmed and tied

2 tablespoons vegetable oil, plus more if needed

½ teaspoon salt, or more to taste

¼ teaspoon freshly ground black pepper, or more to taste

1 large onion, chopped

until the onion is softened, about 5 minutes. Transfer to a 3½-quart slow cooker. Add the beef and its juices. Pour in the 1 cup reserved marinade and the beef broth.

6. Cover and slow-cook until the meat is tender, 7 to 8 hours on low (200°F). Transfer the meat to a serving platter and cover with aluminum foil to keep warm.

7. Skim off the fat from the surface of the cooking liquid. In a blender, purée the cooking liquid and vegetables until smooth. Transfer to a medium saucepan and bring to a boil over medium-high heat. Stir in the gingersnaps and balsamic vinegar. Cook, stirring often, until thickened and reduced to about 2 cups. Season the sauce with additional salt and pepper if desired. Slice the roast across the grain and serve with the gingersnap gravy.

1 medium carrot, finely chopped

1 medium celery rib, finely chopped

½ cup double-strength beef broth, canned or homemade

½ cup crushed gingersnap cookies (about 11 cookies)

2 tablespoons balsamic vinegar

Texas "BBQ" Beef

If you've ever had a craving for mesquite-smoked beef brisket smothered in tangy barbecue sauce, and the weather wasn't cooperating, I have great news. You can enjoy fabulous "barbecued" beef right out of the slow cooker. You can substitute 1½ cups of your favorite commercially made sauce for the Texas BBQ Sauce, but my recipe is so tasty, you should make it from scratch.

Makes 8 sandwiches

1. *For the sauce:* In a medium skillet, melt the butter over medium heat. Add the onion and cook, stirring often, until softened, about 5 minutes. Add the garlic and cook, stirring often, for 1 minute. Transfer to a 3½-quart slow cooker. Stir in the catsup, chili sauce, brown sugar, vinegar, steak sauce, mustard, Worcestershire sauce, and Liquid Smoke.

2. Cut the brisket crosswise into 2 or 3 pieces. Stack the pieces in the slow cooker, cover and slow-cook until the beef is very tender, 9 to 10 hours on low (200°F). Transfer the brisket to a platter and cover with foil to keep warm.

3. Skim the fat from the surface of the sauce. Transfer to a medium saucepan, and bring to a boil over medium heat. Cook, stirring often, until reduced to about 1½ cups, 12 to 15 minutes.

4. Using a sharp carving knife, slice the meat against the grain into thin slices. Place the meat on half the hamburger buns, and top with some of the sauce. Serve as sandwiches, with the remaining sauce passed on the side.

TEXAS BBQ SAUCE

2 tablespoons unsalted butter

1 medium onion, finely chopped

1 clove garlic, minced

½ cup catsup

½ cup chili sauce (such as Heinz 57)

¼ cup packed light brown sugar

¼ cup cider vinegar

1 tablespoon bottled steak sauce

1 tablespoon prepared spicy brown mustard

1 tablespoon Worcestershire sauce

½ teaspoon Liquid Smoke (optional)

1 3½-pound first-cut beef brisket

8 hamburger buns, heated

Ham with Port-Raisin Sauce

The ham's braising liquid is transformed into a garnet sauce studded with raisins. Choose tawny or vintage port, as they are the driest types.

Makes 4 to 6 servings

1. Pierce the ham all over with the tip of a sharp knife.
2. In a 3½-quart slow cooker, combine the port, broth, and water. Add the ham, cover, and slow-cook until a meat thermometer inserted into the center of the ham reads at least 165°F, 4 to 5 hours on low (200°F), or 2 to 3 hours on high (300°F). Turn the ham once during the cooking period for even distribution of flavor.
3. Transfer the ham to a platter and cover with aluminum foil to keep warm. Pour the cooking liquid into a medium saucepan, bring to a boil over high heat, and cook until the cooking liquid has reduced to 2 cups, about 5 minutes. Stir in the raisins, brown sugar, and vinegar, reduce the heat to low, and simmer for 5 minutes. Whisk in the cornstarch mixture and cook until just thickened. Pour the sauce into a sauceboat.
4. Slice the ham and serve with the sauce passed on the side.

Note: "Cure 81" refers to a method of curing that results in a more flavorful, less salty ham. If you can't find a Cure 81 ham, or if you suspect your ham may be salty, blanch the ham before cooking it: Place the ham in a large saucepan of cold water. Over low heat, slowly bring the water just to the simmering point. Drain the ham immediately, and proceed with the recipe.

1 2½-pound boneless smoked ham, preferably "Cure 81" (see Note)

2 cups tawny or vintage port

⅓ cup double-strength beef broth, canned or homemade

⅓ cup water

½ cup dark raisins

2 tablespoons light brown sugar

2 teaspoons red wine vinegar

1 tablespoon cornstarch dissolved in 2 tablespoons cold water

Pork Roast in Chile Verde Sauce

The chili gets its color from tomatillos, small green tomato-like fruits that are difficult to find outside of Hispanic communities. However, green taco sauce, which is made from tomatillos, is readily available.

Makes 4 to 6 servings

2 tablespoons olive oil, divided

1 3-pound bone-in pork loin roast, well trimmed and tied

1/4 teaspoon salt

1/4 teaspoon freshly ground black pepper

1 medium onion, chopped

1 medium Italian frying pepper, seeded and chopped

1 fresh hot green chile pepper (such as jalapeño), seeded and chopped

2 garlic cloves, minced

1 8-ounce bottle green taco sauce

1/2 cup double-strength chicken broth, canned or homemade

2 tablespoons chopped fresh cilantro

1. In a large skillet, heat 1 tablespoon of the oil over medium-high heat. Add the pork roast and cook, turning occasionally, until browned on all sides, about 10 minutes. Transfer the roast to a plate and season with the salt and pepper.

2. Add the remaining 1 tablespoon oil to the skillet and reduce the heat to medium. Add the onion, frying pepper, chile pepper, and garlic. Cook, stirring often, until the onion is softened, about 5 minutes. Transfer to a 3 1/2-quart slow cooker, and stir in the green taco sauce and chicken broth. Place the pork roast on top.

3. Cover and cook until a meat thermometer inserted into the center of the roast reads at least 165°F, 5 to 6 hours on low (200°F), or 2 to 3 hours on high (300°F). Transfer the roast to a platter and cover with foil to keep warm.

4. Skim the fat from the surface of the cooking liquid. Transfer the cooking liquid and solids to a blender, add the cilantro, and blend until smooth. Pour the sauce into a medium saucepan and bring to a boil over medium-high heat. Cook, stirring often, until the sauce is thickened, about 5 minutes.

5. Slice the roast into thick slices. Serve immediately with the sauce passed on the side.

Pork Loin in Milk Sauce

This unusual Tuscan method of cooking pork gives excellent results, as the rich milk seems to seal in the roast's juices even better than more familiar braising liquids. Don't be alarmed if the cooking liquid looks separated—it will all come together in the blender when you make the creamy sauce.

Makes 4 to 6 servings

1 tablespoon unsalted butter

1 tablespoon vegetable oil, plus more if needed

1 3-pound boneless pork loin, well trimmed and tied

1/2 teaspoon salt

1/4 teaspoon freshly ground black pepper

1 medium onion, chopped

1 medium carrot, chopped

2 garlic cloves, chopped

2 cups milk, divided

1/2 teaspoon dried rosemary

1 bay leaf

1. In a large skillet, melt the butter with the oil over medium-high heat. Add the pork roast and cook, turning often, until browned on all sides, about 10 minutes. Transfer the roast to a 3½-quart slow cooker and season with the salt and pepper.

2. Add more oil to the skillet, if necessary, and heat over medium heat. Add the onion and carrot and cook, stirring often, until softened, about 5 minutes. Add the garlic and cook, stirring often, for 1 minute. Add ½ cup of the milk, the rosemary, and bay leaf. Bring just to a simmer, stirring constantly to scrape up the browned bits on the bottom of the skillet with a wooden spoon. Transfer to the slow cooker, and pour in the remaining 1½ cups milk.

3. Cover and slow-cook until the pork is tender, 5 to 6 hours on low (200°F). Transfer the pork to a platter and cover with foil to keep warm.

4. Skim the fat from the surface of the cooking liquid, and discard the bay leaf. In a medium saucepan, bring the cooking liquid to a boil over medium heat. Cook, stirring often, until the sauce has reduced to about 1 cup. Transfer to a blender and process until smooth. Slice the roast, and serve with the sauce passed on the side.

North Carolina Rainy Day "Barbecued" Pork

In the Carolinas, pork is the *only* meat to barbecue (in Texas, it's beef brisket), and vinegar always plays a big part. Here's an indoor version that can be served as a "plate" with coleslaw and baked beans, but also makes a great sandwich.

Makes 8 sandwiches

1. In a large nonreactive bowl, combine the vinegar, onion, Worcestershire sauce, and hot pepper sauce. Add the pork roast, cover, and refrigerate for at least 8 hours, or overnight, turning the pork as often as you remember to do so.

2. Remove the pork from the marinade, scraping the onion off the pork and back into the marinade. Pat the pork roast dry with paper towels. Pour the marinade into a 3½-quart slow cooker and add the Liquid Smoke. Place a collapsible vegetable steamer or a slow cooker meat rack in the slow cooker.

3. In a small bowl, combine the sugar, salt, paprika, and pepper. Rub the pork roast with the spice mixture, and place on the steamer or rack.

4. Cover and slow-cook until the pork is very tender, 7 to 8 hours on low (200°F). Transfer the pork to a cutting board and cover with foil to keep warm.

5. Skim the fat from the surface of the cooking liquid. Stir in the catsup, and pour into a bowl. Using two forks, pull the pork apart into shreds. Serve the pork on the heated buns, passing the sauce on the side to spoon over the sandwiches.

½ cup cider vinegar

1 small onion, chopped

1 teaspoon Worcestershire sauce

1 teaspoon hot pepper sauce

1 3-pound boneless pork shoulder roast (Boston butt), well trimmed and tied

1 teaspoon Liquid Smoke (optional)

1 tablespoon granulated sugar

1 teaspoon salt

1 teaspoon paprika

¼ teaspoon freshly ground black pepper

2 tablespoons catsup

8 hamburger buns, heated

Pork Roast in Orange Sauce

Latin American cooks use sour oranges, a taste I've mimicked by adding a touch of lemon juice to the juice of our sweet oranges.

Makes 4 to 6 servings

1. In a large skillet, heat the oil over medium-high heat. Add the pork loin and cook, until browned on all sides, about 7 minutes. Transfer the pork to a plate and season with the salt and pepper.

2. Add the onion and chile pepper to the skillet, and add more oil if needed. Reduce the heat to medium and cook, stirring often, until the onion is softened, about 5 minutes. Add the garlic and cook, stirring often, for 1 minute. Remove from the heat, and add the orange juice, scraping up the browned bits on the bottom of the pan with a wooden spoon. Transfer to a 3½-quart slow cooker and place the meat on top. Pour in the chicken broth.

3. Cover and slow-cook until the pork is tender, 5 to 6 hours on low (200°F). Transfer the pork to a serving platter and cover with foil to keep warm.

4. Skim the fat from the surface of the cooking liquid. In a medium saucepan, bring the cooking liquid to a simmer over medium heat. In a small bowl, dissolve the cornstarch in the lemon juice, and whisk into the cooking liquid. Stir in the orange zest, and cook just until thickened, about 1 minute.

5. Slice the roast and serve immediately, with the orange sauce passed on the side.

2 tablespoons vegetable oil, plus more if needed

1 3-pound boneless pork loin, well trimmed

¼ teaspoon salt

¼ teaspoon freshly ground black pepper

1 medium onion, chopped

1 fresh hot green chile pepper (such as jalapeño), seeded and minced

1 garlic clove, minced

⅓ cup fresh orange juice

½ cup double-strength chicken broth, homemade or canned

2 teaspoons cornstarch

2 tablespoons fresh lemon juice

Grated zest of 1 orange

Veal Breast Stuffed with Zucchini and Ricotta

The toothsome texture and delicate flavor of the veal is offset by the zesty cheese and vegetable filling. Stuffed veal breast is a labor of love, so I save this recipe for a special Sunday supper menu. I like to add the browned veal bones to my braising liquid for extra flavor, but you can skip this step if you wish.

Serves 4 to 6

2 medium zucchini, shredded

2 teaspoons salt, divided

2 tablespoons olive oil, divided, plus more if needed

2 medium onions, finely chopped, divided

1 garlic clove, minced

3/4 cup fresh bread crumbs

3/4 cup part-skim ricotta cheese

1/3 cup coarsely chopped walnuts

1/4 cup freshly grated imported Parmesan cheese

1 large egg, lightly beaten

1 teaspoon dried basil

1/2 teaspoon freshly ground black pepper, divided

1 3-pound veal breast, boned (bones reserved)

1 medium carrot, chopped

1. In a colander, toss the zucchini and 1 teaspoon of the salt. Let stand until the zucchini gives off its juices, about 1 hour. Rinse the zucchini well under cold running water, and squeeze the excess moisture from the zucchini.

2. In a large skillet, heat 1 tablespoon of the oil over medium heat. Add the grated zucchini, half the chopped onions, and the garlic. Cook, stirring often, until the zucchini begins to stick to the skillet, about 5 minutes. Transfer the zucchini mixture to a large bowl and cool slightly.

3. Beat the bread crumbs, ricotta, walnuts, Parmesan cheese, egg, basil, 1/2 teaspoon of the salt, and 1/4 teaspoon of the pepper into the zucchini; set aside.

4. Position the broiler rack about 6 inches from the source of heat and preheat the broiler. Broil the veal bones, turning once, until browned, about 10 minutes. Transfer the veal bones to a 3 1/2-quart slow cooker.

5. Meanwhile, open out the boned veal, boned side up, on a work surface. Season the veal with the remaining ½ teaspoon salt and ¼ teaspoon pepper. Spread the zucchini filling over the veal, leaving a 1-inch border on all sides. Starting at a short end, roll up the veal. Tie the veal crosswise at 2-inch intervals with kitchen string, tuck in the ends to enclose the filling, and tie the veal lengthwise.

6. In a large skillet, heat the remaining 1 tablespoon oil over medium-high heat. Add the veal and cook, turning occasionally, until browned on all sides, about 10 minutes. Scatter the carrot and remaining chopped onions around the veal and cook, stirring often, until the onion is softened, about 3 minutes. Transfer the browned veal with its juices and the vegetables to the slow cooker. Pour in the chicken broth and wine.

7. Cover and cook until the veal is tender, 6 to 7 hours on low (200°F). Transfer the veal roast to a platter and cover with foil to keep warm. Strain the cooking liquid, and skim the fat from the surface.

8. In a small saucepan, melt the butter over low heat. Whisk in the flour and cook, whisking constantly, until lightly browned, about 2 minutes. Whisk in the cooking liquid and bring to a simmer. Cook until lightly thickened and reduced to about 1½ cups, 6 to 8 minutes. Transfer the sauce to a sauceboat.

9. Slice the veal breast into ¾-inch-thick slices, and serve with the sauce.

continued

½ cup double-strength chicken broth, canned or homemade

½ cup dry white wine

2 tablespoons unsalted butter

2 tablespoons all-purpose flour

Have the butcher bone the veal breast for you, or do it yourself: Using a sharp, thin knife, begin at the thin part of the breast, with the tip of the knife pointing downwards toward the rib bones. Cut the meat away from the bones, peeling the meat back as you proceed. When you reach the breast bone (at the end of the rib bones), turn the breast over, and repeat the procedure on the underside until you meet the breast bone again. Carefully cut the meat off the breast bone, removing the meat in one piece. With a sharp, large knife or a cleaver, cut between the rib bones to make individual ribs. (If your butcher bones the veal breast, ask him to give you the bones too.)

Yankee Corned Beef with
Maple-Mustard Glaze and Winter Vegetables

You'll get incredibly tender corned beef when it's slow-cooked, simmered with onions, carrots, potatoes, and turnips. I cook the cabbage separately, lest its strong flavor overwhelm the others. Since corned beef is notorious for shrinking during cooking, it's best to cook a large cut in a 5-quart cooker (see Note).

Makes 4 to 6 servings

1. In a 5-quart slow cooker, combine the potatoes, carrots, turnips, and onion. Add the corned beef, then pour in the water.

2. Cover and slow-cook until the corned beef is fork-tender, 9 to 11 hours on low (200°F). Using a slotted spoon, transfer the corned beef and vegetables to a large platter, and cover with foil to keep warm.

4 medium boiling potatoes, scrubbed, unpeeled and halved

3 medium carrots, cut into 1½-inch lengths

4 small turnips, scrubbed, unpeeled and halved

1 medium onion, studded with 2 whole cloves

1 4- to 5-pound corned beef brisket, well trimmed

2 cups water

1 medium head green cabbage, cored and cut into 8 wedges

3. Pour the cooking liquid into a large saucepan and bring to a boil over medium-high heat. Add the cabbage wedges, cover, and cook until just tender, 12 to 15 minutes.

4. Meanwhile, position a broiler rack 6 inches from the source of heat and preheat the broiler. In a small bowl, stir together the maple syrup, spicy mustard, and brown sugar until smooth.

5. Place the corned beef on a piece of foil, fat side up, and spread with the brown sugar mixture. Broil, watching carefully, until the corned beef is glazed, about 2 minutes. Return the corned beef to the platter.

6. Using a slotted spoon, transfer the cabbage to the platter. Thinly slice the corned beef on the bias across the grain. Serve immediately, with small bowls of horseradish and mustard.

Note: For a 3½-quart slow cooker, use 2 medium potatoes, 2 medium carrots, 2 small turnips, 1 small onion stuck with 1 whole clove, one 2½-pound corned beef brisket, 2 cups water, 1 small head cabbage, 1 tablespoon syrup, and 1½ teaspoons each mustard and brown sugar. Slow-cook the corned beef for 8 to 10 hours.

2 tablespoons pure maple syrup or pancake syrup

1 tablespoon prepared spicy brown mustard

1 tablespoon light brown sugar

Prepared horseradish and mustard (optional)

Chicken and Turkey

Poultry's popularity has dramatically increased in the last few years, to the point that Americans now eat more chicken and turkey than red meat. However, poultry is one of the easiest things to overcook in a slow cooker, so here are some tips on how to avoid problems.

Cooking a whole chicken is awkward, as the chicken has to tilt on an angle in order to fit into a 3½-quart slow cooker. Also, the whole chickens that look beautiful when sitting in the slow cooker often fall apart easily when transferred to a platter. (An exception is the Soy-Spice Simmered Chicken, because the chicken is trussed so it can be removed more easily from the braising liquid.)

A cut-up chicken is easiest to accommodate in the crockery insert. Cut the chicken into ten pieces: two drumsticks, two thighs, two wings, two breast halves, and the back chopped crosswise into two pieces.

Chicken thighs, at their best when well cooked, are my favorite chicken part to slow-cook on their own. If you like chicken breasts, be careful not to overcook them—four and a half to five hours on low may be sufficient, depending on the size. In any poultry recipe, the white meat takes less time to cook than the dark meat. In order to compensate for this, I always put the dark meat on the bottom of the crockery insert, stacking the white meat on top. As the cooking liquid on the bottom begins to warm, the dark meat will start to cook first, with the breast cooking later as the steam builds in the slow cooker.

Even if you remove the skin when eating poultry, be sure to leave the skin on during slow-cooking. Leaving the skin on during cooking improves the appearance, flavor, and texture. You are not saving any calories by removing the skin before cooking!

Turkey is not just for Thanksgiving anymore, and individual turkey parts can be found in the supermarket. In addition to the turkey recipes in this chapter, thighs are used in Turkey and Hominy Chili (page 58), and drumsticks play a part in Turkey, Escarole, and White Bean Soup (page 46).

The Good Woman's Chicken Pot Roast

In France, this dish is called *Poulet Bonne Femme,* or, literally, The Good Woman's Chicken. It is a good lady (or gentleman), indeed, who creates such a lovely meal from such simple ingredients.

Makes 4 servings

1. In a large skillet, heat the oil over medium-high heat. Add the chicken skin side down, in batches without browning, and cook until the skin is golden brown, about 3 minutes. (Do not turn the chicken.) Transfer the chicken to a plate and season with the salt and pepper. Pour off the fat.

2. Reduce the heat to medium, and melt the butter in the skillet. Add the carrots and onions and cook, stirring, until the onions are lightly browned. Stir in the chicken broth, tarragon, thyme, and bay leaf, and remove from the heat.

3. Place the potatoes on the bottom of the slow cooker and add the vegetable mixture. Stack the chicken in the slow cooker, with the dark meat first and the breast pieces on top.

4. Cover and slow-cook until the chicken is tender, 5 to 6 hours on low (200°F). Using a slotted spoon, transfer the chicken and vegetables to a platter and cover with foil to keep warm.

5. Skim the fat from the surface of the cooking liquid. In a medium saucepan over high heat, bring the cooking liquid to a boil. Cook, stirring often, until reduced to about 1 cup. Pour the sauce

1 tablespoon vegetable oil

1 3½-pound frying chicken, cut up into 10 pieces

½ teaspoon salt

¼ teaspoon freshly ground black pepper

1 tablespoon unsalted butter

8 baby carrots (or 2 medium carrots, cut into ½-inch-thick rounds)

8 small boiling onions (about 8 ounces), peeled

¾ cup double-strength chicken broth, canned or homemade

1 teaspoon dried tarragon

¼ teaspoon dried thyme

1 bay leaf

3 medium boiling potatoes, cut into ½-inch-thick rounds

2 tablespoons chopped fresh parsley, for garnish

over the chicken and vegetables, sprinkle with the parsley, and serve immediately.

Amish Country Chicken "Pot Pie": *To the Amish, a chicken pot pie isn't a pastry dish, but a rich chicken soup with lots of egg noodles. Prepare the recipe through Step 3. Meanwhile, in a large pot of lightly salted boiling water, cook 8 ounces fresh egg noodles until just tender; drain well. Remove the chicken from the broth, pull off and discard the skin, and remove the meat from the bones. Coarsely chop the meat, and return to the slow cooker. Stir in the cooked noodles, 1/2 teaspoon crushed saffron, and the parsley. Serve the "pot pie" in large soup bowls.*

Little Italy Chicken Cacciatore

Chicken cacciatore cooked in a slow cooker is all the better because the chicken and sauce have more of a chance to exchange flavors. It is customary, but not essential, to flavor the tomato sauce with dried mushrooms. If you like, stir half a cup of well-rinsed dried mushrooms into the slow cooker along with the tomatoes; porcini mushrooms are preferred, but Polish mushrooms will do just fine.

Makes 4 servings

1. In a large skillet, heat the oil over medium-high heat. Add the chicken skin side down, in batches without crowding, and cook until the skin is golden brown, about 3 minutes. (Do not turn the chicken.) Transfer the chicken to a plate and season with the salt and pepper.

2. Add the onion and bell pepper to the skillet, and add more oil if necessary. Reduce the heat to low and cook, stirring often, until the onion is softened, about 5 minutes. Add the garlic and cook for 1 minute. Transfer to a 3½-quart slow cooker. Add the tomatoes with their purée, the Italian seasoning, bay leaf, and hot pepper, stirring to break up the tomatoes with the side of a spoon. Arrange the chicken in the slow cooker, with the dark meat on the bottom and the breast meat on top.

3. Cover and slow-cook until the chicken is cooked through, 5 to 6 hours on low (200°F). Stir in the olives.

4. Skim the fat from the surface of the sauce. Serve the chicken on hot cooked spaghetti, with Parmesan cheese passed on the side for sprinkling.

2 tablespoons olive oil, plus more if needed

1 3½-pound frying chicken, cut up into 10 pieces

½ teaspoon salt

¼ teaspoon freshly ground black pepper

1 medium onion, chopped

1 medium green bell pepper, seeded and chopped

1 garlic clove, minced

1 28-ounce can peeled tomatoes in thick tomato purée

2 teaspoons Italian herb seasoning

1 bay leaf

¼ teaspoon crushed hot red pepper

½ cup black Mediterranean olives, pitted and chopped

Hot freshly cooked spaghetti

Freshly grated imported Parmesan cheese

Chicken and Root Vegetable Fricassee

Makes 4 servings

1. In a large dry skillet over medium-high heat, cook the chicken thighs skin side down, in batches without crowding, until the skin is browned, about 3 minutes. Transfer the chicken to a plate and season with the salt and pepper. Pour off all but 2 tablespoons of the fat remaining in the pan.

2. Add the onion to the skillet, and reduce the heat to medium. Cook, stirring often, until softened, about 4 minutes. Transfer to a 3½-quart slow cooker. Add the turnips, carrot, parsnip, celery root, and tarragon and stir well.

3. Place the chicken thighs on top of the vegetables. Pour in the chicken broth, wine, and water.

4. Cover and slow-cook until the chicken is cooked through, 5 to 6 hours on low (200°F). Using a slotted spoon, transfer the chicken and vegetables to a serving bowl, and cover with aluminum foil to keep warm. Skim the fat from the surface of the cooking liquid.

5. In a medium saucepan, melt the butter over low heat. Add the flour and cook, whisking constantly without browning, for 1 minute. Whisk in the cooking liquid and heavy cream and bring to a boil. Cook, whisking often, until thickened, about 5 minutes. Pour the sauce over the chicken and vegetables, sprinkle with chives, and serve immediately.

6 chicken thighs (about 2 pounds)

½ teaspoon salt

¼ teaspoon freshly ground black pepper

1 medium onion, chopped

2 medium turnips, scrubbed, unpeeled, and cut into ½-inch-thick rounds

1 carrot, cut into ½-inch-thick rounds

1 parsnip, cut into ½-inch-thick rounds

1 small knob celery root (celeriac), pared, quartered, and cut into ½-inch-thick slices

1 teaspoon dried tarragon

1 cup double-strength chicken broth, canned or homemade

½ cup dry white wine or vermouth

¼ cup water

2 tablespoons unsalted butter

2 tablespoons all-purpose flour

½ cup heavy cream

Chopped fresh chives or parsley, for garnish

Moroccan Chicken and Vegetable Stew

This North African stew of tender chicken thighs with chunks of vegetables produces a substantial amount of fragrant spiced broth to spoon generously over a bed of couscous. My friends and I like to eat this North African style, eschewing forks and using our impeccably clean hands.

Makes 4 to 6 servings

1. Cut the acorn squash crosswise into ¾-inch-thick rings and scoop out the seeds. Cut the rings into quarters and pare off the skin.

2. In a small bowl, combine ½ teaspoon of the salt, the cinnamon, ginger, turmeric, and pepper.

3. In a 3½-quart slow cooker, combine the acorn squash, carrots, onion, and garlic. Sprinkle half the spice mixture over the vegetables. Sprinkle the remaining spice mixture over the chicken thighs, and arrange the thighs over the vegetables. Pour in the chicken broth, cover, and slow-cook until the chicken shows no sign of pink at the bone when prodded with the tip of a sharp knife, 5 to 6 hours on low (200°F). During the last 30 minutes of cooking, add the garbanzo beans and raisins.

4. Meanwhile, about 10 minutes before the chicken is done, prepare the couscous. In a medium saucepan, combine the water, butter, and remaining ¾ teaspoon salt and bring to a boil. Stir in

1 acorn squash (about 1 pound)

1¼ teaspoons salt, divided

½ teaspoon ground cinnamon

½ teaspoon ground ginger

½ teaspoon ground turmeric

½ teaspoon freshly ground black pepper

2 medium carrots, cut into ½-inch-thick rounds

1 onion, thinly sliced

2 garlic cloves, minced

6 chicken thighs (about 2 pounds), skin removed if desired

1¾ cups double-strength chicken broth, canned or homemade

1 15-ounce can garbanzo beans (chickpeas), drained and rinsed

⅓ cup dark raisins

2¾ cups water

the couscous. Remove from the heat, cover tightly, and let stand until the liquid is absorbed, about 5 minutes.

5. Fluff the couscous with a fork. Heap the hot couscous on a warmed platter. Spoon the chicken, vegetables, and broth over the couscous and serve immediately, with the Moroccan Hot Sauce served on the side.

3 tablespoons unsalted butter

1 10-ounce package quick-cooking couscous

Moroccan Hot Sauce (recipe follows)

Moroccan Hot Sauce

To add authentic fire to your Moroccan Chicken and Vegetable Stew, drizzle on small amounts of this incendiary sauce.

Makes about ½ cup

1. Sprinkle the garlic with the salt. Using a sharp knife, chop and then mash the salted garlic to make a paste. Scrape the garlic into a small bowl. Stir in the reserved cooking liquid, the crushed hot red pepper, and lemon juice.

2. Use a small spoon to drizzle the sauce over the Moroccan Chicken and Vegetable Stew.

2 garlic cloves, crushed

¼ teaspoon salt, preferably coarse

⅓ cup reserved cooking liquid from Moroccan Chicken and Vegetable Stew (page 150)

1 tablespoon crushed hot red pepper

1 teaspoon lemon juice

Chicken with Mushrooms and Artichokes in Red Wine Sauce

Students of French cuisine will recognize this as Coq au Vin, Slow Cooker-Style. For any cooking, pick a hearty, dry red wine such as a Zinfandel. Lighter wines, like Beaujolais, are best enjoyed as beverages. It doesn't have to be a pricey wine, but remember that the better the wine, the better the sauce.

Makes 4 servings

1. In a large skillet over medium heat, cook the bacon until crisp. Using a slotted spoon, transfer the bacon to paper towels to drain, leaving the bacon fat in the skillet.

2. Add the chicken pieces skin side down, in batches without crowding, and cook until the skin is golden brown, about 3 minutes. (Do not turn the chicken.) Transfer the browned chicken to a plate and season with the salt and pepper. Pour off all but 2 tablespoons of the fat from the pan.

3. Add the mushrooms, onion, and carrots to the skillet and cook, stirring often, until the mushrooms have given off their liquid and are beginning to brown, about 7 minutes. Add the garlic and stir for 1 minute. Stir in the wine, parsley, thyme, and bay leaf. Bring to a boil, scraping up the browned bits on the bottom of the skillet. Stir in the broth and reserved bacon. Transfer the mixture to a 3½-quart slow cooker.

4. Stack the chicken in the slow cooker, with the dark meat first

4 strips bacon, cut into 1-inch-wide pieces

1 3½-pound frying chicken, cut up into 10 pieces

¼ teaspoon salt

¼ teaspoon freshly ground black pepper

10 ounces fresh mushrooms, quartered

1 medium onion, chopped

2 medium carrots, chopped

2 garlic cloves, minced

½ cup dry red wine, such as Zinfandel

2 tablespoons chopped fresh parsley

½ teaspoon dried thyme

1 bay leaf

½ cup double-strength chicken broth, canned or homemade

1 10-ounce package frozen artichoke hearts, defrosted

2 tablespoons unsalted butter

2 tablespoons all-purpose flour

and the breast pieces on top. Cover and slow-cook until the chicken is tender, 5 to 6 hours on low (200°F). About an hour before the chicken is done, add the artichokes.

5. Using a slotted spoon, transfer the chicken and vegetables to a platter, and cover with aluminum foil to keep warm. Skim the fat off the surface of the cooking liquid.

6. In a medium saucepan, melt the butter over low heat. Add the flour and cook, whisking constantly without browning, about 1 minute. Whisk in the cooking liquid and bring to a boil. Increase the heat to high and cook, stirring often, until thickened and reduced to about 1½ cups. Pour the sauce over the chicken and vegetables, and serve immediately.

African Marinated Chicken in Onion Sauce

Known as *yassa,* this is the national dish of Senegal, and is served over rice. As the onions cook, they melt down to create a "sauce" for the piquant chicken. Add as much cayenne pepper as you wish—the dish should be as spicy as you can stand it.

Makes 4 servings

5 large onions, thinly sliced

4 garlic cloves, minced

1/4 cup lemon juice

1 teaspoon salt

1/4 teaspoon cayenne pepper, or more to taste

1 3 1/2-pound frying chicken, cut up into 10 pieces

2 tablespoons vegetable oil

4 cups hot freshly cooked rice

1. In a large nonreactive bowl, combine the onions, garlic, lemon juice, salt, and cayenne pepper. Add the chicken and toss to coat well. Cover with plastic wrap and refrigerate overnight, turning the chicken in the marinade as often as you remember to do so.

2. Remove the chicken from the marinade and pat dry with paper towels. Pour the marinade, with the onions, into a 3 1/2 -quart slow cooker.

3. In a large skillet, heat the oil over medium-high heat. Add the chicken skin side down, in batches without crowding, and cook until the skin is golden brown, about 3 minutes. (Do not turn the chicken.) Stack the chicken in the slow cooker, dark meat first, then the breast pieces.

4. Cover and slow-cook until the chicken is tender, 5 to 6 hours on low (200°F). Using kitchen tongs, transfer the chicken to a serving bowl, and cover with foil to keep warm.

5. Transfer the onions and cooking liquid to a large skillet and bring to a boil over high heat. Cook, stirring often, until the liquid has totally evaporated, 10 to 15 minutes. Spoon the onions over the chicken and serve immediately with the hot cooked rice.

Basque Chicken and Rice Casserole

Chicken, ham, and rice is a popular combination in Spain. In fact, with the addition of shellfish and peas, this could be paella (see below). Be sure to use converted long-grain rice, as regular rice will slow-cook into a mushy mess. For a winning meal-in-a-pot, this casserole can't be beat.

Serves 4 to 6

1. In a large skillet, heat the oil over medium-high heat. Add the chicken pieces skin side down, in batches without crowding, and cook until the skin is brown, about 3 minutes. (Do not turn the chicken.) Transfer the chicken pieces to a plate and sprinkle with the lemon juice. Pour off all but 2 tablespoons of the fat.

2. Add the ham, onion, red bell pepper, and garlic to the skillet, reduce the heat to medium, and cook, stirring often, until the onion is softened, about 5 minutes. Transfer to a lightly oiled 3½-quart slow cooker.

3. Stir in the water, chicken broth, oregano, salt, saffron, and crushed red pepper. Stir in the rice. Stack the chicken in the slow cooker, dark meat first, then the breast pieces on top. Cover and slow-cook until the rice is tender and the chicken is cooked through, 5 to 6 hours on low (200°F). Serve directly from the slow cooker.

Slow-Cooked Paella: *During the last 15 minutes of cooking, stir in 1 cup defrosted petite peas and ½ pound shelled medium shrimp. Cover and continue slow-cooking until the shrimp have turned pink and firm.*

1 tablespoon olive oil

1 3½-pound frying chicken, cut up into 10 pieces

Juice of 1 lemon

5 ounces smoked ham, cut into ¼-inch cubes (about 1 cup)

1 medium onion, chopped

1 medium red bell pepper, seeded and chopped

3 garlic cloves, minced

2½ cups water

1¾ cups double-strength chicken broth, canned or homemade

1 teaspoon dried oregano

¾ teaspoon salt

¼ teaspoon crushed saffron threads

⅛ teaspoon crushed hot red pepper

2 cups converted long-grain rice

Soy-Spice Simmered Chicken

This soy sauce, Chinese spice, and sugar mixture can be used to simmer poultry or red meats to juicy perfection. As the cooking liquid imparts a reddish tone to the meats, the Chinese call this "red cooking." You can save and refrigerate the leftover poaching liquid and use it again; just be sure to bring the liquid to a boil on top of the stove before using. Soy-Spice Simmered Chicken is best at room temperature, and it improves in flavor if allowed to chill overnight. Serve with Chinese Cabbage and Peanut Slaw (page 227) for a great picnic.

Makes 4 servings

1. Using butcher's twine, tie the chicken drumsticks together. Tie the chicken wings to the body.

2. In a 3½-quart slow cooker, combine both soy sauces, the chicken broth, rice wine, brown sugar, ginger, Szechuan peppercorns, star anise, and cinnamon stick, stirring to dissolve the sugar. Place the chicken in the slow cooker, drumstick end down.

3. Cover and cook until a meat thermometer inserted in the thickest part of the thigh, not touching the bone, reads at least 170°F, 5 to 6 hours on low (200°F). Halfway through the cooking time, turn the chicken breast side down in the cooking liquid so that it colors evenly.

4. Using two wooden spoons, carefully transfer the chicken to a plate. Cool completely, wrap tightly in plastic wrap, and refrigerate

1 3½-pound chicken

1 cup soy sauce (preferably Japanese, such as Kikkoman)

½ cup Chinese dark soy sauce (see Note)

½ cup double-strength chicken broth

¼ cup rice wine or dry sherry

¼ cup light brown sugar

2 teaspoons finely chopped fresh ginger

1 teaspoon Szechuan peppercorns (see Note)

1 star anise pod or ¼ teaspoon fennel seed (see Note)

1 cinnamon stick

overnight. Remove from the refrigerator 1 hour before serving. (The leftover cooking liquid can be saved for future use; cover it tightly and refrigerate for up to 1 month. Bring to a boil before using.)

Note: Dark soy sauce, Szechuan peppercorns, and star anise are available in Oriental grocery stores and many supermarkets. If dark soy sauce is unavailable, substitute ½ cup regular soy sauce plus 2 tablespoons molasses, and reduce the brown sugar to 2 tablespoons.

Soy-Spice Simmered Drumsticks, Thighs, or Breasts: *Simmer individual chicken drumsticks or thighs in the sauce for 5 to 6 hours on low (200°F). Chicken breasts will cook in 4 to 5 hours.*

Chicken Stew with Spicy Peanut Sauce

The seasonings may seem exotic, but they come together to create a delicious dish. To keep the zucchini from overcooking, cook it separately and stir it in at the end of the cooking time.

Makes 4 servings

1. In a large skillet, heat 1 tablespoon of the oil over medium-high heat. Add the chicken skin side down, in batches without crowding, and cook until the skin is golden brown, about 3 minutes. (Do not turn the chicken.) Transfer to a plate and season with the salt. Pour off all but 1 tablespoon of the fat in the skillet.

2. Add the onion to the skillet. Reduce the heat to medium and cook, stirring often, until softened. Add the garlic and cook, stirring often, for 1 minute. Transfer to a 3½-quart slow cooker. Stir in the carrots, tomato sauce, curry powder, and cayenne pepper. Stack the chicken in the slow cooker, dark meat on the bottom and breast meat on top. Cover and slow-cook until the chicken is cooked through, 5 to 6 hours on low (200°F).

3. Meanwhile, in a medium skillet, heat the remaining 1 tablespoon oil over medium heat. Add the zucchini and cook, stirring occasionally, until lightly browned, about 5 minutes. Transfer the zucchini to paper towels to drain.

4. In a small bowl, combine the yogurt and peanut butter. Stir the mixture into the slow cooker, add the browned zucchini, and cook just until heated through, about 5 minutes. Serve directly from the slow cooker.

2 tablespoons vegetable oil, divided, plus more if needed

1 3½-pound chicken, cut up into 10 pieces

½ teaspoon salt

1 medium onion, chopped

2 garlic cloves, minced

2 medium carrots, cut into ½-inch-thick rounds

1 8-ounce can tomato sauce

1 teaspoon curry powder

¼ teaspoon cayenne pepper

2 medium zucchini, cut into ½-inch-thick rounds

½ cup plain yogurt

½ cup unsalted, sugar-free peanut butter

Turkey Breast Tonnato

In Italy, this dish is made with braised veal roast, but I find that boneless turkey breast makes an admirable substitute. The dish should be made a day ahead so the flavors can mellow, making it perfect for carefree summer entertaining.

Makes 4 servings

1. Starting at a short end, roll up the turkey breast into a cylinder and tie in several places with butcher's twine.
2. In a 3½-quart slow cooker, combine the wine, water, onion, carrot, celery, salt, and pepper. Place the turkey breast in the slow cooker.
3. Cover and slow-cook until a meat thermometer inserted in the center of the turkey breast reads 165°F, 4 to 5 hours on low (200°F). Uncover and let the turkey breast cool completely in the liquid, then discard the cooking liquid.
4. In a blender or food processor, combine the tuna, lemon juice, and anchovies. With the machine on, gradually add the olive oil and process to form a smooth sauce.
5. Slice the turkey breast into ½-inch slices. Arrange the slices, overlapping, on a serving platter. Spread the tuna sauce evenly over the turkey slices. Cover the platter tightly with plastic wrap and refrigerate until well chilled, at least 4 hours or overnight.
6. Just before serving, sprinkle the turkey with the capers, and garnish with the lemon slices.

1 2-pound boneless skinless turkey breast

½ cup dry white wine

½ cup water

1 small onion, chopped

1 small carrot, finely chopped

1 small celery rib, finely chopped

½ teaspoon salt

¼ teaspoon freshly ground black pepper

1 6½-ounce can tuna, preferably imported Italian tuna packed in olive oil, drained

2 tablespoons lemon juice

4 anchovy fillets, rinsed

¾ cup olive oil

1 tablespoon capers, rinsed

1 medium lemon, sliced, for garnish

Turkey Breast Saltimbocca

Turkey breast rolled with prosciutto and sage will "jump into your mouth," which is the literal translation of the Italian term *saltimbocca*. I serve this as a summertime entrée with a sliced tomato and mozzarella salad, and pass the Italian Green Herb Sauce on the side.

Makes 4 servings

1. Place the turkey breast between two sheets of plastic wrap. Using a flat meat pounder or a rolling pin, pound the breast to an even ¾-inch thickness. Remove the top sheet of plastic and cover the turkey with overlapping slices of the prosciutto, leaving a 1-inch border on all sides. Sprinkle with the sage. Starting at a short end, roll up the breast jelly-roll fashion, and tie in several places with string. Season with the salt and pepper.

2. In a 3½-quart slow cooker, combine the white wine and chicken broth. Add the turkey breast, cover, and slow-cook until a meat thermometer inserted in the center of the turkey breast reads 170°F, 4 to 5 hours on low (200°F).

3. Let the turkey breast cool in the cooking liquid. Discard the cooking liquid.

4. Wrap the turkey breast tightly in plastic wrap and refrigerate overnight. Remove the string and cut into ½-inch-thick slices. Serve at cool room temperature, with the green sauce passed on the side.

1 2-pound boneless skinless turkey breast

2 ounces sliced prosciutto

6 fresh sage leaves, chopped, or ½ teaspoon crumbled dried sage

½ teaspoon salt

¼ teaspoon freshly ground black pepper

½ cup dry white wine

¼ cup double-strength chicken broth, canned or homemade

Italian Green Herb Sauce (page 93)

Green Peppers with Turkey-Corn Stuffing

These green peppers are filled with a ground turkey and corn mixture that has a hint of chili flavoring. The peppers are simmered with stewed tomatoes, and the cooking liquid easily becomes the accompanying sauce when puréed in the blender. This sauce is also great over hot cooked rice.

Makes 4 servings

1 14½-ounce can stewed tomatoes

½ cup Italian-seasoned dry bread crumbs

1 large egg

1 small onion, finely chopped

1 garlic clove, minced

2 teaspoons chili powder

1 teaspoon salt

1 pound ground turkey

½ cup fresh or defrosted frozen corn kernels

4 small green bell peppers (about 4 ounces each), tops cut off, seeds and ribs removed

1. Drain the stewed tomatoes, reserving the juices. Measure ¼ cup of the juices and set aside. Place the stewed tomatoes and the remaining juices in a 3½-quart slow cooker.

2. In a medium bowl, combine the reserved ¼ cup tomato juices, the bread crumbs, egg, onion, garlic, chili powder, and salt and mix well. Add the ground turkey and corn and mix well. Mound the turkey mixture into the peppers. Arrange three peppers in the slow cooker, and balance the fourth on top of them.

3. Cover and slow-cook until the turkey stuffing is cooked through, 5 to 6 hours on low (200°F). Transfer the peppers to a platter and cover with aluminum foil to keep warm.

4. Transfer the tomatoes and cooking liquid to a blender and process until smooth. Pour the sauce into a sauceboat, and serve with the peppers.

Turkey and Corn Pudding

Here's a great recipe for your leftovers file. Don't let day-after turkey get you down—use it in your slow cooker to make this homey casserole.

1. In a medium skillet, melt the butter over medium heat. Add the onion and cook, stirring often, until softened, about 4 minutes. Transfer to a medium bowl.

2. Whisk the creamed corn, eggs, evaporated milk, flour, salt, and pepper into the onion until combined. Stir in the chopped turkey. Transfer to a lightly buttered 3½-quart slow cooker.

3. Cover and slow-cook until a knife inserted into the center of the pudding comes out almost clean, 2½ to 3 hours on high (300°F).

4. Sprinkle the top of the pudding with the cheese, cover, and cook until melted, about 5 minutes. Serve directly from the slow cooker.

Variation: *Add 1 fresh hot chile pepper (such as jalapeño), seeded and minced, and 2 garlic cloves, minced, to the cooked onions and cook for 1 minute longer, stirring often.*

1 tablespoon unsalted butter

1 medium onion, chopped

1 16-ounce can cream-style corn

4 large eggs

½ cup evaporated milk

⅓ cup all-purpose flour

½ teaspoon salt

¼ teaspoon freshly ground black pepper

2 cups chopped cooked turkey or chicken

½ cup shredded sharp Cheddar cheese

Vegetables and Other Side Dishes

The biggest advantage to cooking side dishes in the slow cooker is that it allows the cook breathing space to concentrate on other parts of the menu. In addition, there are many dishes that are improved when given the slow-cooked treatment.

Lots of vegetables are just as delicious when cooked beyond the crisp-tender stage. Down-Home Collard Greens, Sweet and Sour Red Cabbage, Southern-Style Smothered Green Beans, and Fennel Pizzaiola are just a few that feature meltingly tender, flavorful vegetables. Root vegetables, such as Baby Carrots with Port Wine Glaze and Orange-Tarragon Beets, are easier to cook to the desired stage of doneness than by other methods, since it is difficult to overcook such vegetables in the slow cooker. And if you are looking for condiments to add zest to your main dishes, try Pineapple and Macadamia Chutney.

Sometimes, especially during the holiday season, it doesn't seem as if there are enough pots, pans, or stove burners to get you through your menu. Then I often call my slow cooker into action to prepare side dishes, especially if there are other items on the bill of fare that require the stove top or oven. Cranberry-Pear-Walnut Sauce, Herbed Thanksgiving Stuffing, Wild Rice, Apricot, and Pecan Dressing, and Louisiana Yam and Pineapple Pudding are four slow-cooked recipes that are sure to become holiday favorites in your household.

Greek Stuffed Artichokes with Egg-Lemon Sauce

I grew up not far from Castroville, California, the Artichoke Capital of the World, and remember springtime lunches when we gorged on boiled artichokes and mayonnaise. (The local farmstands sold them for 10 cents each!) Filled to the brim with parsley, garlic, and mint, then braised in a lemon-scented broth that later becomes a delicate sauce for dipping the tender leaves, these could be served for a light lunch or as a first course for a special dinner.

Makes 4 servings

1 large lemon, halved

4 medium artichokes

2 cups chopped fresh parsley

2 tablespoons chopped fresh mint or 2 teaspoons dried mint

2 garlic cloves, minced

1/2 teaspoon salt

1/4 teaspoon freshly ground black pepper

1 1/3 cups double-strength chicken broth, homemade or canned

1 1/3 cups water

3 large egg yolks

2 teaspoons cornstarch

1. Squeeze a lemon half into a medium bowl of cold water. Using a sharp knife, cut off the top 1 inch of one of the artichokes. Cut off the stem so the artichoke will stand upright. Spread open the outer leaves to reveal the tender, light green, inner cone of leaves. Using a dessert spoon, scoop out this cone of leaves, including the hairy thistle underneath. Immediately drop the artichoke into the lemon water to avoid discoloration. Repeat with the remaining artichokes.

2. In a medium bowl, combine the parsley, mint, garlic, salt, and pepper. Drain the artichokes and stuff the centers with the herb mixture.

3. Stand the artichokes up in a 5-quart slow cooker. Pour in the chicken broth and water. Squeeze the remaining lemon half over the artichokes, then drop the half into the cooking liquid.

4. Cover and cook until a leaf can be easily pulled from an artichoke, about 4 hours on high (300°F). Using a slotted spoon, transfer the artichokes to a platter and cover with foil to keep warm.

5. Strain the cooking liquid into a medium saucepan. In a medium bowl, whisk together the egg yolks and cornstarch. Gradually whisk the cooking liquid into the yolk mixture and then pour back into the saucepan. Cook over low heat, stirring constantly with a wooden spoon, until the sauce lightly coats the spoon, about 5 minutes. Do not let the sauce come near a boil, or it will curdle. (A thermometer inserted into the sauce should read 175°F.)

6. Pour the sauce into four small bowls. Serve the artichokes with the sauce. To eat, dip the leaves into the sauce, then scoop up the herb stuffing.

Ratatouille Niçoise

Having almost scorched many a ratatouille in my pre–slow cooker days, I swear by the crockery pot method. Great ratatouille should never be soupy, and the best Provençal chefs cook down the vegetable juices to a glaze, as in this recipe. Enjoy hot ratatouille as a side dish for grilled salmon or lamb, or serve it at room temperature on a bed of greens as a salad.

1 medium eggplant (about 1¼ pounds), cut into ¾-inch cubes

2 medium zucchini, cut into ½-inch cubes

1¾ teaspoons salt, divided

6 tablespoons olive oil, divided

2 medium onions, chopped

1 medium green bell pepper, seeded and chopped

3 garlic cloves, minced

1 28-ounce can peeled tomatoes in thick tomato purée

1 teaspoon dried basil

¾ teaspoon dried thyme

¾ teaspoon dried rosemary

¼ teaspoon crushed hot red pepper

1. In a large colander, toss the eggplant and zucchini cubes with 1 teaspoon of the salt. Let stand until the vegetables release their juices, about 1 hour. Rinse well under cold running water to remove the salt, then drain well. Squeeze the vegetables, a handful at a time, to remove excess moisture, and pat dry with paper towels.

2. In a large skillet, heat 3 tablespoons of the oil over medium-high heat. Cook the eggplant/zucchini mixture in two batches, stirring occasionally, until lightly browned, about 5 minutes. Using a slotted spoon, transfer the eggplant and zucchini to the slow cooker.

3. Add the remaining 3 tablespoons oil to the skillet. Add the onions and bell pepper, reduce the heat to medium, and cook, stirring often, until the onions are softened, about 5 minutes. Add the garlic and cook, stirring often, for 1 minute. Add the tomatoes with their purée, the basil, thyme, rosemary, remaining ¾ teaspoon salt, and the crushed red pepper. Bring to a simmer, breaking up the tomatoes with a spoon. Transfer to the slow cooker. Cover and slow-cook until the vegetables are tender, 6 to 7 hours on low (200°F).

4. Pour the ratatouille into a colander set over a large bowl and let drain for 10 minutes. Transfer the ratatouille to a serving bowl.

5. Pour the drained cooking liquid into a medium saucepan. Bring to a boil over high heat and cook, stirring often to avoid scorching, until thickened and reduced to about ½ cup, 10 to 15 minutes. Stir the reduced liquid into the ratatouille. Serve hot, warm, or at room temperature. (If possible, let the ratatouille cook to room temperature, cover, and refrigerate overnight to allow the flavors to blend. Reheat, if desired.)

Romanian Vegetable Casserole

Ghivisu is the name of this classic Romanian stew, created with an abundance of vegetables. This version is based on my friend Maria Laghi's family recipe. Maria says you can add or subtract any number of vegetables, with two caveats in mind: First, avoid beets, as their color will bleed onto the other vegetables. Secondly, be sure that any vegetable you choose is cut smaller than 1 inch square so it will cook to tenderness. While I normally serve *ghivisu* as an accompaniment to grilled sausages or chicken, it can be a satisfying vegetarian main course, too.

Makes 6 to 8 servings

1 medium eggplant (about 1 pound), cut into 1-inch cubes

2 medium zucchini, cut into 1/2-inch-thick rounds

2 teaspoons salt, divided

3/4 cup olive oil

3 garlic cloves, minced

1 tablespoon Dijon mustard

1 1/2 teaspoons marjoram

1/2 teaspoon crushed red pepper

2 medium boiling potatoes, cut into 1/2-inch-thick slices

2 medium carrots, cut into 1/2-inch-thick rounds

2 medium celery ribs, cut into 1/2-inch-thick slices

2 medium onions, sliced

1/2 small head cabbage, cored and cut crosswise into 1/2-inch strips

1 15-ounce can peeled Italian tomatoes, drained and chopped

1. In a large colander, toss the eggplant and zucchini with 1 teaspoon of the salt. Let stand until the vegetables release their juices, about 1 hour. Rinse the vegetables well under cold running water to remove the salt. Squeeze the vegetables, a handful at a time, to remove excess moisture, and pat dry with paper towels.

2. Meanwhile, in a small bowl, combine the olive oil, garlic, mustard, marjoram, the remaining 1 teaspoon salt, and the crushed red pepper.

3. In a 3 1/2-quart slow cooker, layer the vegetables in the following order, drizzling each layer with some of the olive oil mixture: potatoes, eggplant/zucchini, carrots, celery, onions, cabbage, and tomatoes.

4. Cover and cook until all the vegetables are tender, 7 to 8 hours on low (200°F). Stir well before serving.

Fennel Pizzaiola

Fennel is a vegetable that Americans should learn to appreciate as much as the Italians do. It has a crisp texture like celery, and just the barest hint of licorice flavor. I like to serve this as a side dish for a simple pork roast, but it makes an excellent pasta sauce, too.

Makes 4 servings

1. With a sharp knife, cut off the feathery fennel fronds. Finely chop 2 tablespoons of the fronds; discard the remainder. Cover the chopped fronds with plastic wrap and refrigerate until ready to serve.

2. Cut the fennel in half lengthwise, and cut out the thick core from the bottom. Cut the fennel bulb and stalks crosswise into ½-inch-thick pieces. Place the sliced fennel in a 3½-quart slow cooker.

3. In a small skillet, heat the oil over medium heat. Add the onion and cook, stirring often, until softened, about 4 minutes. Add the garlic and stir for 1 minute. Transfer to the slow cooker. Stir in the tomatoes, rosemary, salt, and pepper. Cover and slow-cook until the fennel is tender, 5 to 6 hours on low (200°F).

4. Just before serving, stir in the olives, and sprinkle with the reserved fennel fronds and the grated cheese.

1 medium bulb fennel (about 1 pound)

1 tablespoon olive oil

1 large onion, chopped

2 garlic cloves, minced

1 28-ounce can peeled Italian tomatoes, drained and chopped

1 teaspoon dried rosemary

¼ teaspoon salt

⅛ teaspoon freshly ground black pepper

½ cup black Mediterranean olives, pitted and coarsely chopped

3 tablespoons freshly grated imported Parmesan cheese

Italian Spinach and Cheese Timbale

Unmolded onto a platter, this is a great-looking, great-tasting side dish. Freshly grated Italian Parmesan cheese always has the best flavor; look for the words "Parmigiano-Reggiano" printed on the rind. (If you buy grated Parmesan, be sure it is the real thing.) Ersatz "imported" Parmesan-style cheese may actually be from Argentina, and is inferior. As for the already-grated variety you find unrefrigerated on the grocery shelves, the less said the better.

Makes 4 to 6 servings

1. Generously butter the inside of a 1-quart soufflé dish. Dust the inside of the dish evenly with the bread crumbs, tilting the dish to be sure the entire surface is covered. Tap out the excess crumbs. Place a collapsible vegetable steamer or a slow-cooker meat rack in a 5-quart slow cooker, and pour in 2 cups hot water. Preheat the slow cooker on high (300°F) while making the timbale.

2. In a medium saucepan, melt the butter over low heat. Add the onion and cook, covered, until softened, about 5 minutes. Add the garlic and cook, uncovered, stirring often, for 1 minute. Sprinkle with the flour and stir for 1 minute, without browning. Gradually stir in the half-and-half. Bring to a simmer, reduce the heat to low, and simmer for 5 minutes. Stir in the Parmesan cheese.

3. In a medium bowl, whisk the egg yolks. Gradually whisk the hot cheese sauce into the yolks. Stir in the spinach, salt, pepper, and nutmeg.

2 tablespoons dried Italian-seasoned bread crumbs

3 tablespoons unsalted butter

1 medium onion, finely chopped

1 garlic clove, minced

3 tablespoons all-purpose flour

1 cup half-and-half or milk

1/3 cup freshly grated imported Parmesan cheese

3 large eggs, separated, at room temperature

1 10-ounce package frozen chopped spinach, defrosted and squeezed to remove excess moisture

1/2 teaspoon salt

1/8 teaspoon freshly ground black pepper

Pinch of freshly grated nutmeg

1/8 teaspoon cream of tartar

4. In a grease-free medium bowl, using a hand-held electric mixer set at low speed, beat the egg whites until foamy. Add the cream of tartar, increase the speed to high, and beat just until stiff peaks form. Stir about one fourth of the beaten whites into the spinach mixture to lighten it, then fold in the remainder. Pour the mixture into the prepared dish. Cover tightly with foil.

5. Place the dish on the steamer or rack in the slow cooker. Cover and slow-cook until a knife inserted in the center of the timbale comes out clean, about 3 hours. (Do not cook on low [200°F] for a longer period of time.)

6. Let the timbale stand 5 minutes before unmolding. Run a sharp knife around the inside of the mold, then invert onto a platter. Cut into wedges to serve.

Orange-Tarragon Beets

Even before root vegetables were fashionable, I loved the vibrant color and sweet flavor of beets. (I may be the only child in history who asked his mom to make beets.) These make a zesty, hot side dish for grilled chicken, but are also wonderful chilled and dressed with olive oil as a salad.

8 medium beets (about 2 pounds), peeled and cut into 1/2-inch-thick rounds

1/3 cup freshly squeezed orange juice

2 tablespoons raspberry or red wine vinegar

Grated zest of 1 large orange

1 teaspoon dried tarragon

1/2 teaspoon salt

1/4 teaspoon freshly ground black pepper

1. In a 3 1/2-quart slow cooker, combine the beets, orange juice, vinegar, orange zest, tarragon, salt, and pepper. Cover and slow-cook, stirring twice, until the beets are tender, 5 to 6 hours on low (200°F).

2. Using a slotted spoon, transfer the sliced beets to a serving bowl. Serve immediately.

Orange-Tarragon Beet Salad: *Chill the beets in the cooking liquid. Drain the beets, and toss with 1/3 cup olive oil and 1/3 cup coarsely chopped walnuts.*

Scalloped Summer Squash

While zucchini and other summer squash are good cooked crisp-tender, they are also enjoyable when meltingly tender, as in this crumb-topped casserole.

Makes 6 to 8 servings

1. In a large colander, combine the zucchini slices with ½ teaspoon of the salt. Let stand until the zucchini gives off its juices, about 30 minutes. Rinse well under cold running water to remove the salt, drain, and pat dry with paper towels.

2. In a large skillet, heat the oil over medium heat. Add the onion and red bell pepper and cook, stirring often, until softened, about 5 minutes. Add the garlic and cook, stirring often, for 1 minute. Remove from the heat, add the zucchini, and mix well.

3. In a medium bowl, mix the bread crumbs, Parmesan cheese, Italian seasoning, the remaining ½ teaspoon salt, and the pepper.

4. Place half of the zucchini mixture in a buttered 3½-quart slow cooker. Sprinkle with half of the crumb mixture. Top with the remaining zucchini mixture, then sprinkle with the remaining crumbs. Dot the top of the crumbs with the butter.

5. Cover and slow-cook until the zucchini is tender, 4 to 5 hours on low (200°F). Serve directly from the slow cooker.

6 medium zucchini or other summer squash (about 2 pounds), cut into ½-inch-thick rounds

1 teaspoon salt, divided

2 tablespoons olive oil

1 medium onion, chopped

1 medium red bell pepper, seeded and chopped

1 garlic clove, minced

1 cup fresh bread crumbs

⅓ cup freshly grated imported Parmesan cheese

1 teaspoon Italian herb seasoning

¼ teaspoon freshly ground black pepper

1 tablespoon unsalted butter, cut into small cubes

Baby Carrots with Port Wine Glaze

Candied carrots took a place of honor at many of my family's special meals. In my slow-cooked version, the carrots are infused with a port wine–beef broth glaze. Baby carrots are not the sole property of expensive specialty grocers anymore, and my supermarket even carries them prepeeled! If you can't get them, however, cut regular carrots into sticks about 2 inches long by ½ inch wide.

Makes 4 to 6 servings

1. In a 3½-quart slow cooker, combine the carrots, beef broth, port wine, butter, brown sugar, and pepper. Cover and slow-cook, stirring occasionally, until the carrots are tender, 4½ to 6 hours on low (200°F). (The exact timing will depend on the thickness of the carrots.)

2. Turn the heat to high (300°F) and stir in the cornstarch mixture. Cook, uncovered, until the glaze has thickened, about 5 minutes. Stir to coat the carrots with the glaze.

3. Transfer the carrots to a warmed serving dish and serve immediately.

1 pound baby carrots, peeled

¼ cup double-strength beef broth, homemade or canned

¼ cup tawny or vintage port wine

1 tablespoon unsalted butter

1 tablespoon light brown sugar

⅛ teaspoon freshly ground black pepper

1 tablespoon cornstarch dissolved in 1 tablespoon cold water

Sweet and Sour Red Cabbage

My maternal grandmother was born in Liechtenstein, the tiny principality nestled between Germany, Switzerland, and Austria. She always seemed to have something delicious simmering on the back of the stove, and often it was her sweet and sour cabbage, which goes especially well with other Middle European dishes like Erna's Sauerbraten (page 132). The slow cooker makes red cabbage the leisurely, old-fashioned way, and the cabbage is all the better for it.

Makes 6 servings

1. In a large skillet, melt the butter over medium-high heat. Add the onion and cook, stirring often, until lightly browned, about 5 minutes. Transfer to a 3½-quart slow cooker. Stir in the beef broth, vinegar, brown sugar, salt, thyme, bay leaf, and pepper. Add the cabbage and stir well.

2. Cover and slow-cook, stirring once or twice, until the cabbage is very tender, 4 to 5 hours on low (200°F). During the last hour of cooking, stir in the apple and raisins.

3. Using a slotted spoon, transfer to a warmed serving dish. Serve immediately.

2 tablespoons unsalted butter

1 medium onion, chopped

½ cup double-strength beef broth, canned or homemade

¼ cup red wine vinegar

¼ cup light brown sugar

½ teaspoon salt

½ teaspoon dried thyme

1 bay leaf

¼ teaspoon freshly ground black pepper

1 small head cabbage, cored and cut into ¼-inch-thick strips

1 Granny Smith apple, peeled, cored, and chopped

⅓ cup dark raisins

Down-Home Collard Greens

As any Southern cook will testify, the longer and more gently collard greens cook, the better they are, making them a prime candidate for the slow cooker. These are a meaty version to served with Sour Cream Corn Bread (page 222). You can substitute mustard, dandelion, turnip, or kale, or use a combination. Whatever variety you choose, rinse them well, as greens tend to be very sandy.

Makes 4 to 6 servings

1 cup double-strength beef broth, canned or homemade

1 cup water

2 smoked ham hocks (about 9 ounces each)

2 garlic cloves, minced

2 tablespoons cider vinegar

1 teaspoon sugar

½ teaspoon crushed red pepper

3 pounds collard greens, well rinsed, thick stems trimmed off and discarded, cut crosswise into ½-inch-thick strips

Salt to taste

1. In a large pot, combine the broth, water, ham hocks, garlic, vinegar, sugar, and red pepper and bring to a boil over medium-high heat. Add the collard greens in batches, covering the pan and waiting for each batch to wilt before adding the next batch. Transfer to a 3½-quart slow cooker.

2. Cover and cook until the greens are very tender, 4 to 5 hours on low (200°F). Remove the ham hocks from the greens, and remove and discard the skin. Remove the meat from the bones, coarsely chop the meat, and return to the slow cooker. Season the greens with salt to taste.

3. If serving as a side dish, drain the greens, reserving the flavorful cooking liquids—(called "pot liquor")—and serve the greens and pot liquor separately. If serving as a chunky soup, ladle the greens and pot liquor together into deep bowls.

Season the greens with salt after they have cooked, to compensate for the salt that the ham hocks will release into the broth.

Southern-Style Smothered Green Beans

Southern cooks don't cotton much to crisp vegetables, and they have a way with long-cooked green beans, simmered with bacon and onions. While the beans admittedly lose their color, they are permeated with smokey flavor. A sprinkling of fresh sweet red pepper pretties them up.

Makes 8 to 12 servings

1. In a large skillet over medium heat, cook the bacon, stirring often, until crisp and browned, about 5 minutes. Using a slotted spoon, transfer the bacon to paper towels to drain. Pour off all but 2 tablespoons of fat from the skillet.

2. Add the onion to the skillet. Cook, stirring often, until lightly browned, about 5 minutes. Remove from the heat.

3. In a 3½-quart slow cooker, combine the green beans with half the cooked bacon, the cooked onion, water, salt, and pepper. Cover and slow-cook until the green beans are very tender, about 5 hours on low (200°F). During the last hour of cooking, stir in the red bell pepper, vinegar, and sugar.

4. Transfer the beans to a warm serving dish, sprinkle with the remaining cooked bacon, and serve immediately.

6 strips bacon, cut into 1-inch-wide pieces

1 medium onion, chopped

1½ pounds fresh green beans, trimmed and cut into 1-inch lengths

1 cup water

½ teaspoon salt

¼ teaspoon freshly ground black pepper

1 small red bell pepper, seeded and finely chopped

1 tablespoon cider vinegar

1 teaspoon sugar

Louisiana Yam and Pineapple Pudding

This delectable side dish almost outshined the turkey at one of my Thanksgiving meals! Shredded sweet yams are blended with crushed pineapple to make a melt-in-your-mouth treat that would also be great with baked ham. Cooking the yams in the slow cooker frees the oven for other dishes.

Makes 8 to 12 servings

1. In a buttered 3½-quart slow cooker, combine the sweet potatoes, crushed pineapple with its juice, the evaporated milk, brown sugar, butter, eggs, cinnamon, and nutmeg.

2. Cover and slow-cook, stirring about every 1½ hours, until the sweet potatoes are meltingly tender, 7 to 8 hours on low (200°F). The pudding may appear curdled at first, but it will come together with longer cooking and stirring.

3. Serve hot, warm, or at room temperature.

Spiked Sweet Potato Pudding: *Stir ¼ cup dark rum, Cognac, or bourbon into the pudding just before serving.*

While Louisiana yams and sweet potatoes can be substituted for each other, they are not the same thing. Louisiana yams are orange-fleshed with dark skins. Sweet potatoes have creamy yellow flesh and lighter skins. Ironically, they are less sweet than Louisiana yams. A true yam is not a potato at all, but a starchy African tuber related to cassava.

3 pounds Louisiana yams, peeled and shredded

2 8-ounce cans crushed pineapple in unsweetened juice

1 12-ounce can evaporated milk

1¼ cups packed light brown sugar

6 tablespoons unsalted butter, cut into ½-inch cubes

3 large eggs, beaten

1 teaspoon ground cinnamon

½ teaspoon ground nutmeg

Potatoes Euphoria

I do not name this recipe lightly. It has the best elements of your favorite potato dishes—the melting texture of mashed potatoes, the creaminess of scalloped potatoes, and the tang of sour cream–topped baked potatoes. It is so tempting that it is one of those recipes for which an exact serving estimate is impossible to give.

Makes 1 to 6 servings, depending on how much you like potatoes

4 scallions, finely chopped

2 garlic cloves, minced

1 teaspoon salt

1/4 teaspoon freshly ground black pepper

8 medium boiling potatoes (about 2 pounds), scrubbed and sliced into 1/8-inch-thick rounds

8 ounces cream cheese, cut into 1-inch cubes

1. In a small bowl, combine the scallions and garlic. In another small bowl, combine the salt and pepper.

2. In a well-buttered 3 1/2-quart slow cooker, layer one fourth of the sliced potatoes. Sprinkle with about 1/4 teaspoon of the salt and pepper, and top with one third of the cheese cubes and then one third of the scallion mixture. Make a second layer of potatoes, sprinkle with about 1/4 teaspoon of the salt and pepper, and top with half the remaining cheese and scallion mixtures. Repeat with a third layer of potatoes, sprinkle with another 1/4 teaspoon of the salt and pepper, and top with the remaining cheese and scallion mixtures. Make a final layer of potatoes and sprinkle with the remaining salt and pepper.

3. Cover and slow-cook for 2 hours on high (300°F). Stir the potatoes to distribute the melting cheese, cover, and continue slow-cooking until the potatoes are very tender, about 1 hour longer.

4. Stir the potatoes well to mash slightly, and serve immediately.

Herbed Thanksgiving Stuffing

As the author of *The Turkey Cookbook,* I can "talk turkey" with authority. I am a firm believer of not stuffing the bird with bread stuffing. (I stuff mine with a light flavoring mixture of vegetables and herbs.) Bread stuffing adds extra poundage and bulk to the bird, making it difficult to judge the roasting time accurately. To solve the problem of where to cook the stuffing, simply make it in the slow cooker. For the best flavor, use a homemade turkey stock, made from the turkey giblets simmered in some store-bought chicken broth with an onion and a carrot.

Makes 10 to 12 servings

1. In a large skillet, melt the butter over medium heat. Add the onions, celery, and apple. Cook, stirring often, until the onions are softened, about 10 minutes. Remove from the heat and stir in the parsley, rosemary, thyme, marjoram, sage, salt, and pepper.

2. In a large bowl, mix the bread cubes with the onion mixture. Tossing the bread cubes, add the turkey broth to moisten. Pack the stuffing lightly into a buttered 3½-quart slow cooker.

3. Cover and slow-cook on high (300°F) for 1 hour. Reduce the heat to low (200°F) and slow-cook until heated through, 3 to 4 hours. (The slow cooker will keep the dressing at serving temperature for up to 3 hours.)

8 tablespoons (1 stick) unsalted butter

2 large onions, chopped

3 medium celery ribs, chopped

1 medium Granny Smith apple, chopped

½ cup chopped fresh parsley

1½ teaspoons dried rosemary

1½ teaspoons dried thyme

1½ teaspoons dried marjoram

1½ teaspoons crumbled sage

1½ teaspoons salt

½ teaspoon freshly ground black pepper

12 packed cups 1-inch cubes of stale Italian or French bread (about 1 pound)

1½ cups turkey or chicken stock, preferably homemade (page 182)

Sausage Thanksgiving Stuffing: *In a large skillet, cook 1 pound bulk pork sausage (or 1 pound turkey sausages, casings removed) over medium heat, stirring often to break up lumps, until the meat shows no sign of pink and is cooked through, about 8 minutes. Drain off excess fat. Stir the cooked sausage into the Thanksgiving Stuffing during the last hour of cooking.*

Mushroom Thanksgiving Stuffing: *In a large skillet, melt 4 tablespoons butter over medium heat. Add 1½ pounds fresh mushrooms, sliced, and cook, stirring often, until the mushrooms have given off their liquid and are beginning to brown, about 8 minutes. Stir the cooked mushrooms into the Thanksgiving Stuffing during the last hour of cooking.*

Wild Rice, Apricot, and Pecan Dressing

Makes 8 to 10 servings

1. In a large skillet, melt the butter over low heat. Add the shallots and celery, cover, and cook, stirring often, until the celery is softened, about 5 minutes. Transfer to a buttered 3½-quart slow cooker.

2. Stir in the turkey stock, wild rice, thyme, bay leaf, salt, and pepper. Cover and slow-cook, stirring occasionally, until the rice is tender, 4 to 5 hours on high (300°F). Wild rice is a very unpredictable grain, so allow the longest cooking estimate to be sure it is cooked to your liking; once the rice is cooked, turn the heat to low (200°F) to keep warm.

3. Meanwhile, in a small bowl, soak the apricots in the Cognac for at least 1 hour, to plump.

4. When the rice is tender, stir in the apricots, their soaking liquid, and the pecans. (The slow cooker will keep the wild rice dressing at serving temperature for up to 3 hours.)

Note: To make Turkey Stock, follow the recipe for Double-Strength Chicken Stock (page 30), substituting 3 pounds turkey necks or giblets, chopped into 2-inch pieces, for the chicken necks or backs. Or make a quick turkey stock by simmering your turkey's giblets with 4½ cups canned chicken broth, 1 medium onion, and 1 medium carrot (both chopped) for 1 hour.

4 tablespoons unsalted butter

4 shallots, finely chopped

1 medium celery rib, finely chopped

4 cups turkey stock (see Note) or canned chicken broth

2 cups wild rice, rinsed and drained

1 teaspoon dried thyme

1 bay leaf

1 teaspoon salt

¼ teaspoon freshly grated black pepper

6 ounces dried apricots, chopped

¼ cup Cognac, brandy, or apple juice

1½ cups toasted pecans (about 6 ounces), coarsely chopped (page 202)

Gingered Apple Butter

Apple butter is probably the quintessential slow-cooker recipe, as even in conventional cooking, it must be cooked for hours without scorching. The slow cooker eliminates the worry, making an incredibly dense butter that you'd never get on a stovetop. Since the apple butter must cook for 18 to 20 hours, start it before going to bed. Jonathans, MacIntosh, or Rome apples all make excellent apple butter. During apple season, I go to the farmers' market to get the best unwaxed apples and fresh-squeezed cider. Don't peel the apples, as the pectin in the peels will help set the butter.

Makes about 2 pints

4 pounds cooking apples, unpeeled, cored and quartered

1⅓ cups packed light brown sugar

1 cup freshly squeezed apple cider

Grated zest and juice of 1 lemon

3 tablespoons grated fresh ginger

1. The night before, in a 3½-quart slow cooker, combine the apples, brown sugar, apple cider, and lemon zest and juice. Cover and slow-cook until the apples are very, very soft, 8 to 10 hours on low (200°F).

2. The next day, stir in the grated ginger. Increase the heat to high (300°F), uncover, and cook, stirring occasionally, until the mixture has reduced to about 3 cups, 8 to 10 hours.

3. Using a rubber spatula, rub the apple butter through a wire strainer set over a bowl to remove the apple peels.

4. Spoon the warm apple butter into hot sterilized jars. Screw on the two-piece lids and let stand at room temperature 8 hours, or overnight; refrigerate. (The canned apple butter will keep, refrigerated, for up to 6 months.)

Pineapple and Macadamia Chutney

Cooking pineapple chutney in a slow cooker "candies" the fruit in the spiced brown sugar syrup, infusing it in a way I never get with quicker cooking methods. I like to use a fruit-flavored vinegar, such as raspberry, but cider vinegar will do. Pineapple chutney should not be served only with curries—try it with grilled pork chops.

Makes about 2 cups

1. Using a large sharp knife, cut off the pineapple's crown, and discard. Cut off the bottom of the pineapple so that it will sit upright on your work surface. Cutting from the top of the pineapple to the bottom, cut off the thick peel in slabs and discard. Cut out the "eyes" of the pineapple. (Because they run in rows, you can cut out a few at once, instead of one at a time.) Quarter the pineapple lengthwise. Trim off and discard the core from each quarter. Cut each quarter lengthwise into thirds, then crosswise into 1-inch-wide chunks.

2. In a 3½-quart slow cooker, combine the brown sugar, vinegar, onion, chile pepper, garlic, ginger, and cinnamon stick. Stir in the chopped pineapple. Cover and slow-cook until simmering, about 1½ hours on high (300°F). Uncover and cook, stirring occasionally (if possible), until the liquid is reduced to a syrup, about 3 hours more.

3. Stir in the macadamia nuts, and cool completely before serving. (The chutney can be covered and refrigerated for up to a week.

1 large pineapple

1 cup packed light brown sugar

½ cup raspberry or cider vinegar

1 small onion, finely chopped

1 fresh hot green chile pepper (such as jalapeño), seeded and minced

1 garlic clove, minced

1 tablespoon grated fresh ginger

1 cinnamon stick

½ cup macadamia nuts (about 2 ounces), rinsed of salt and coarsely chopped

For longer storage, spoon the hot chutney into hot sterilized canning jars. Screw on the two-piece lids and let stand at room temperature overnight. The canned chutney will keep, refrigerated, for up to 6 months.)

Fresh ginger rarely has to be pared, especially when it is to be grated. If the ginger seems old and the skin is tough, it can be peeled with a vegetable peeler.

Cranberry-Pear-Walnut Sauce

Made on top of the stove, cranberry sauce can scorch easily. But, with the slow cooker, I can let the cranberries and pears blend their flavors without fear of frying.

Makes about 3 cups

1. In a 3½-quart slow cooker, combine the cranberries, pears, sugar, raisins, water, and orange zest. Cover and slow-cook until most of the cranberries have popped and the pears are tender, about 2 hours on high (300°F). Stir in the walnuts.

2. Transfer the sauce to a bowl, cover, and let cool. Refrigerate until chilled and thickened, at least 4 hours or overnight. (The sauce can be covered and refrigerated for up to a week.)

1 12-ounce bag cranberries, rinsed and picked over

3 medium Bosc pears, peeled, cored, and chopped into ½-inch cubes

1½ cups sugar

1 cup dark raisins

¼ cup water

Grated zest of 1 orange

1 cup coarsely chopped toasted walnuts

Desserts

Of all the different kinds of foods I have slow-cooked, my desserts always get the most pleased, surprised response: "You made THIS in a slow cooker?" It's easy to picture a slow cooker creating tender pot roasts and tasty stews, but incredibly smooth crème caramel? Fruity blueberry grunt with a sweet dumpling topping? A gorgeous molded persimmon gingerbread?

Some slow-cooker manufacturers recommend "baking" cakes in the appliance, but you either have to cover the top of the batter with paper towels to protect it from dripping condensation, or buy one of their special baking pans that keeps the moisture out. In either case, the resulting "baked" dessert has an undesirable, rubbery texture. There are so many good desserts that benefit from being cooked in a slow cooker, why bother with something that's only so-so?

After burning and ruining too many batches of stovetop cooked mincemeat, I tried simmering mincemeat in the slow cooker, and sweet success was mine! Apple-Pear Meatless Mincemeat is included in this collection, along with detailed instructions on how to turn it into a golden-brown pie.

At every Christmas dinner, I serve my all-time favorite dessert, my grandmother's steamed persimmon gingerbread. One year the batter was all made, already in the pudding mold, and I turned to the stove to put on a pot of water to cook it. But all of the burners were taken with other pots that could not be interrupted. I had the inspiration to use the slow cooker, and the pudding turned out beautifully. Now I always slow-cook my holiday puddings.

I have added other steamed delights to Grandma's gingerbread, and Chocolate-Pecan Pudding and Figgy Pudding Noël are just two suggestions. They are not soft, like puddings, but firm enough to slice like a cake. If you want a spoonable pudding, try Honeyed Apple-Orange Pudding or Lemon-Raspberry Pudding Cake.

You will need a 10-cup (2½-quart) fluted tube pudding mold with lids for some of these recipes. (If yours is missing a lid, cover tightly with aluminum foil.) These molds fit perfectly into a 5-quart slow cooker. Do not make your steamed desserts in an empty coffee can, as they did in the old days. Coffee cans are meant to hold coffee, not to cook in! As the metal heats up, it is possible that toxic materials could leak into your food. None of the coffee companies I talked to recommend cooking in their cans.

Have you ever had your custards weep and separate? The cause is an oven temperature that is too high. The proteins in eggs separate into solids and liquids if heated beyond 350°F. I tested this theory in a slow cooker (since the slow cooker never goes above 300°F) and was rewarded with the most luxuriously textured custard. I provide two recipes to support my experiment— Crème Caramel Valencia and Pumpkin Crème Brûlée.

One last note: It is very important to cook the desserts at the temperatures listed in each recipe. The steamed puddings, for example, will not rise properly if cooked on low instead of high.

Blueberry Grunt

Stewed berries topped with a sweet dumpling crust make an old-fashioned dessert. Blackberries, raspberries, or huckleberries, either fresh or frozen, all work equally well.

Makes 4 servings

1. In a 3½-quart slow cooker, combine the blueberries, the ½ cup granulated sugar, the water, and tapioca. Cover and slow-cook until the berries have formed a thick sauce, 5 to 6 hours on low (200°F).

2. In a medium bowl, whisk the flour, the remaining 2 tablespoons granulated sugar, the baking powder, and salt to combine. Using a pastry blender or two knives, cut in the butter until the mixture resembles coarse meal. In a small bowl, beat the milk and egg together. Stir into the flour mixture to form a soft dough.

3. Turn the heat to high (300°F). Drop the dough by tablespoons on top of the blueberries. Cover and slow-cook until the topping is firm and a toothpick inserted in the center comes out clean, about 30 minutes. Sprinkle the dumplings with the brown sugar.

4. Let the grunt stand for 5 minutes before serving, then spoon into individual bowls.

How did such an ambrosial dish get such an unattractive monicker? One story explains that the dessert was originally prepared on top of the stove in a heavy iron pot, which elicited a "grunt" from the cook when lifted from the fire.

2 pints fresh or frozen blueberries

½ cup plus 2 tablespoons sugar, divided

½ cup water (use warm water if using frozen berries)

2 tablespoons instant tapioca

2 cups all-purpose flour

2½ teaspoons baking powder

½ teaspoon salt

5 tablespoons chilled unsalted butter, cut into ½-inch cubes

½ cup milk

1 large egg

2 tablespoons light brown sugar

Lemon-Raspberry Pudding Cake

This pudding cake makes its own lemony sauce, so the dessert needs no adornment other than a simple sprinkling of confectioners' sugar.

Makes 4 servings

1. Spread the raspberries over the bottom of a 1½-quart soufflé dish.

2. In a medium bowl, whisk the sugar and flour to combine. Add the milk, egg yolks, lemon zest and juice, and the melted butter, and whisk just until combined.

3. In a grease-free, medium bowl, using a hand-held electric mixer set at low speed, beat the egg whites until foamy. Increase the speed to high and beat just until stiff peaks form. Fold the whites into the lemon mixture. Pour into the soufflé dish and cover tightly with aluminum foil.

4. Place a collapsible vegetable steamer or slow-cooker meat rack in the bottom of a 5-quart slow cooker. Place the soufflé dish on the steamer or rack. Pour in enough hot water to come 1 inch up the side of the dish. Cover and slow-cook on high (300°F) until the top of the cake springs back when lightly pressed, about 2 hours.

5. Sift confectioners' sugar over the top of the cake to garnish. Serve the pudding warm, spooned into individual bowls.

½ pint fresh raspberries

½ cup sugar

3 tablespoons all-purpose flour

1 cup milk

2 large eggs, separated, at room temperature

Grated zest of 1 large lemon

3 tablespoons fresh lemon juice

2 tablespoons unsalted butter, melted

Confectioners' sugar

Grandma Edith's Persimmon Gingerbread Pudding

When I was growing up in California, my grandmother's neighbors would present her with a bushel of persimmons each December. So, our Christmas dessert collection always featured her warm persimmon pudding served with brandied eggnog sauce. I have kept the tradition alive, creating the pudding each year from a treasured, dog-eared recipe card.

Makes 6 to 8 servings

1. *Make the persimmon pudding:* Generously butter the inside of a 2½-quart fluted tube pudding mold. Dust the inside of the mold lightly with flour, and tap out the excess.

2. In a food processor or blender, purée the unpeeled persimmons. You should have 1 cup purée. Add the sugar, milk, butter, and egg and process until well mixed. Transfer the persimmon mixture to a bowl.

3. Sift together the flour, baking soda, ginger, salt, cinnamon, mustard, and cloves. Add to the persimmon mixture and whisk until smooth. Whisk in the chopped crystallized ginger. Scrape the batter into the prepared pudding mold.

4. Cover the mold with its lid or foil. Place in a 5-quart slow cooker and pour 2 cups of hot water around the mold. Cover and slow-cook until a toothpick inserted into the center of the pudding comes out clean, about 3 hours on high (300°F). (Do not cook on low for a longer period of time.)

PERSIMMON GINGERBREAD
PUDDING

2 well-ripened medium Hachiya persimmons, stems discarded

1 cup sugar

½ cup milk

2 tablespoons unsalted butter, melted

1 large egg

1 cup all-purpose flour

2 teaspoons baking soda

1 teaspoon ground ginger

½ teaspoon salt

½ teaspoon ground cinnamon

¼ teaspoon dry mustard

¼ teaspoon ground cloves

½ cup finely chopped crystallized ginger (optional)

5. *Meanwhile, make the eggnog sauce:* In a chilled medium bowl, beat the cream and sugar until stiff. Using a rubber spatula, fold in the eggnog and rum. Pour the sauce into a sauceboat, cover, and chill until ready to serve.

6. Unmold the pudding onto a platter. Slice and serve warm with the sauce served on the side.

There are two varieties of persimmons available, each with different characteristics that make it impossible to use them interchangeably with guaranteed success. Fuyu persimmons are squat-shaped and should be eaten crisp-ripe. (Serve them, thinly sliced, in a spinach salad with a soy-rice vinegar dressing, sprinkled with sesame seeds.) Hachiya persimmons are longer and plumper. These are the persimmons to use in cooking, and should be ripened until very soft and the skin takes on an almost translucent appearance. To be sure your Hachiya persimmons will be at this soft-ripe stage for your recipe, buy them a few days ahead, and let ripen in a closed paper bag at room temperature. Ripened persimmons will keep in the refrigerator for 3 days, or purée the persimmons, skin and all, and freeze for up to 2 months.

EGGNOG SAUCE

1 cup heavy cream

2 tablespoons sugar

⅓ cup prepared dairy eggnog

1 tablespoon dark rum, brandy, or bourbon (optional)

Strawberry-Strawberry Cheesecake

Everyone loves strawberry-topped cheesecake, but this one gets strawberries inside, too, turning it a lovely pink shade. My friends couldn't believe that this sensational dessert came from a slow cooker.

Makes 8 servings

1. In a medium bowl, combine the crumbs, the 2 tablespoons sugar, and the melted butter. Press the mixture over the bottom and ½ inch up the sides of a buttered 8-inch springform pan. Cover and freeze until the crust is set, about 30 minutes.

2. In a medium bowl, using a hand-held electric mixer set at medium-high speed, beat the cream cheese until very smooth. Add the remaining ½ cup sugar and beat well. Beat in the eggs, one at a time, then beat in the cornstarch. Beat in the strawberry preserves. Pour the mixture into the prepared crust and cover tightly with aluminum foil.

3. Place a collapsible vegetable steamer or a slow-cooker meat rack in a 5-quart slow cooker. Place the cheesecake on top of the steamer or rack. Cover and slow-cook until the sides of the cheesecake have puffed, 2½ to 3 hours on high (300°F). The center of the cheesecake may seem underdone, but it will firm upon chilling. (Do not slow-cook on low for a longer period of time.)

4. Let the cheesecake stand in the slow cooker until cool enough to remove. Then refrigerate, covered, until firm, at least 4 hours, or overnight.

¾ cup graham cracker crumbs (from about 6 whole crackers)

½ cup plus 2 tablespoons sugar, divided

4 tablespoons unsalted butter, melted

1 pound cream cheese, well softened

2 large eggs, at room temperature

1 tablespoon cornstarch

½ cup strawberry preserves

⅓ cup red currant jelly

1 pint fresh strawberries, rinsed, stemmed, and patted dry

Spiced Pumpkin Cake

What's a holiday dinner without a pumpkin dessert? Serve this warm pudding with old-fashioned applesauce (made the day before in your slow cooker) or whipped cream.

Makes 6 to 8 servings

1. Generously butter the inside of a 2½-quart fluted tube pudding mold. Dust the inside of the mold with flour, tapping out excess.

2. In a large bowl, using a hand-held electric mixer set at high speed, beat the butter until creamy. Add the brown sugar and beat until light in color and texture, about 2 minutes. Add the eggs one at a time, beating well after each addition. Beat in the pumpkin purée and evaporated milk.

3. Sift the flour, baking powder, cinnamon, allspice, ginger, and cloves together onto a piece of waxed paper. On low speed, add the flour mixture to the pumpkin mixture and beat just until combined, scraping down the sides of the bowl with a rubber spatula as necessary. Transfer the batter to the prepared mold.

4. Cover the mold with its lid or foil. Place the mold in a 5-quart slow cooker and pour 2 cups of hot water around the mold. Cover and slow-cook until a toothpick inserted into the center of the mold comes out clean, about 2½ hours on high (300°F). (Do not cook on low for a longer period of time.) Let the cake stand for 5 minutes before unmolding.

5. Unmold the cake onto a platter. Slice and serve warm, with the applesauce or whipped cream passed on the side.

8 tablespoons (1 stick) unsalted butter, softened

1 cup packed light brown sugar, rubbed through a strainer to remove lumps

3 large eggs, at room temperature

1¼ cups canned pumpkin purée

¼ cup evaporated milk

1½ cups bleached all-purpose flour

1½ teaspoons baking powder

1 teaspoon ground cinnamon

1 teaspoon ground allspice

½ teaspoon ground ginger

¼ teaspoon ground cloves

2 cups Autumntime Applesauce (page 231), or sweetened whipped cream

Hot Fudge Spooncake

Ever since I was a kid, I have been partial to those seemingly magical desserts that divide themselves into warm cake and smooth, spoonable sauce. Happily, they are just the thing for the slow-cooker enthusiast. Here's a chocolate variety that I find irresistible with or without a scoop of vanilla ice cream.

Makes 4 to 6 servings

1. Sift 1 cup of the brown sugar, the flour, the 3 tablespoons cocoa powder, the baking powder, and salt together through a strainer into a medium bowl, rubbing the brown sugar through to remove any lumps. Whisk in the milk, melted butter, and vanilla. Spread evenly over the bottom of a 3½-quart slow cooker.

2. Mix together the remaining ¾ cup brown sugar and ¼ cup cocoa powder. Sprinkle evenly over the top of the batter. Pour in the hot water, but do not stir.

3. Cover and slow-cook until a toothpick inserted 1-inch deep into the center of the cake comes out clean, about 2 hours on high (300°F). (Do not cook on low for a longer period of time.)

4. Spoon the warm pudding into individual bowls, served with scoops of vanilla ice cream if desired.

1¾ cups packed light brown sugar, divided

1 cup all-purpose flour

¼ cup plus 3 tablespoons nonalkalized cocoa powder, such as Hershey's

2 teaspoons baking powder

¼ teaspoon salt

½ cup milk

2 tablespoons unsalted butter, melted

½ teaspoon vanilla extract

1¾ cups hot water

Vanilla ice cream (optional)

Karren's Bourbon Street Bread Pudding

Karren Hecht, my first sous-chef in my catering business and a talented hostess without peer, finally shared this incredibly rich and delicious bread pudding recipe with me after years of cajoling, and I've adapted it to slow-cooking. It is equally good warm, cold, or at room temperature.

Makes 4 servings

1. In a small bowl, combine the raisins and bourbon and let stand until the raisins are plumped, at least 1 hour. Or microwave the raisins and bourbon on high (100 percent) for 1 minute.

2. In a medium saucepan, heat the milk and butter over medium heat, stirring often, until the butter has melted. Remove from the heat.

3. In a medium bowl, whisk the sugar, eggs, and vanilla until combined. Gradually whisk in the hot milk mixture. Stir in the raisins with the bourbon.

4. Place the bread cubes in a lightly buttered 2½-quart soufflé dish. Pour the egg mixture over the cubes. Cover the dish with foil.

5. Place a collapsible vegetable steamer or a slow-cooker meat rack in the bottom of a 5-quart slow cooker and pour in 2 cups hot water. Place the soufflé dish in the slow cooker. Cover and slow-cook until the pudding is puffed and a knife inserted in the center comes out almost clean, 3 hours on high (300°F).

6. Serve warm or at room temperature. (The pudding will sink upon cooling.)

⅓ cup raisins

3 tablespoons bourbon or apple cider

3 cups milk

12 tablespoons (1½ sticks) unsalted butter, cut up

1 cup sugar

2 large eggs

¾ teaspoon vanilla extract

8 cups 1-inch cubes of French or Italian bread (about 7 ounces) (I keep the crust on)

Steamed Chocolate-Pecan Pudding

Here's another moist, light-as-a-cloud pudding. A dollop of whipped cream is the perfect accompaniment, and fresh raspberries add color and tang.

Makes 6 to 8 servings

1. Generously butter the inside of a 2½-quart fluted tube pudding mold. Dust the inside of the mold with flour, and tap out the excess.

2. In the top part of a double boiler, set over hot, not simmering, water, melt the chocolate, stirring often. Remove the top part of the double boiler from the heat and cool the chocolate, stirring often, until tepid, about 10 minutes.

3. In a medium bowl, using a hand-held electric mixer set at high speed, beat the egg yolks and sugar until a thick ribbon forms when the beaters are lifted 2 inches from the surface, about 2 minutes. Beat in the tepid chocolate and the vanilla.

4. Sift the flour, baking powder, baking soda, and salt together onto a piece of waxed paper. On low speed, beat the flour mixture into the chocolate mixture, just until combined, scraping down the sides of the bowl with a rubber spatula as necessary. (The batter will be thick.)

5. In a medium bowl, using a hand-held electric mixer with clean dry beaters set at low speed, beat the egg whites until foamy.

6 ounces semisweet chocolate, finely chopped

6 large eggs, separated at room temperature

1 cup sugar

½ teaspoon vanilla extract

¼ cup all-purpose flour

½ teaspoon baking powder

½ teaspoon baking soda

¼ teaspoon salt

1 cup coarsely chopped pecans (about 4 ounces)

1 tablespoon unsweetened cocoa powder

Sweetened whipped cream, for garnish

Fresh raspberries, for garnish

Increase the speed to high and beat just until the egg whites form soft peaks. Whisk about one-fourth of the egg whites into the chocolate batter to loosen, then fold in the remaining whites.

6. In a small bowl, toss the pecans with the cocoa to coat. Stir into the batter. Scrape the batter into the prepared mold.

7. Cover the mold with its lid or foil. Place the mold in a 5-quart slow cooker and pour 2 cups of hot water around the mold. Cover and slow-cook until a toothpick inserted into the center of the mold comes out clean, about 3 hours on high (300°F). (Do not cook on low heat for a longer period of time.)

8. Unmold the pudding onto a platter. Slice, and garnish each serving with a dollop of whipped cream and raspberries.

Double-Crust Mincemeat Pie

Warm mincemeat pie, fresh out of the oven and topped with vanilla ice cream, is, for me, one of Christmas's finest indulgences. The pastry recipe makes enough extra dough to cut into festive shapes to adorn the top crust. You can use small cookie cutters, or cut them freehand with a sharp paring knife.

Makes one 10-inch pie

1. In a medium bowl, combine the flour and salt. Using a pastry blender or two knives, cut in the shortening and butter until the mixture resembles coarse meal, with a few pieces of fat that are the size of small peas. Tossing the mixture with a fork, gradually sprinkle in the ½ cup iced water, mixing with the fork, until just moistened and the mixture holds together when pinched between your thumb and forefinger. You may have to add more iced water, 1 tablespoon at a time. Gather the dough into two thick flat disks, one twice as large as the other. Wrap each disk in waxed paper and refrigerate for at least 1 hour, or up to 2 days.

2. Position a rack in the bottom third of the oven and preheat the oven to 425°F.

3. On a lightly floured work surface, roll out the larger disk of dough into a 14-inch circle about ⅛ inch thick. Line a 10-inch pie pan with the dough. Trim the excess dough, leaving a 1-inch border around the edges of the pan. Fill the pastry-lined pan with the mincemeat.

3 cups all-purpose flour

½ teaspoon salt

¾ cup chilled vegetable shortening

6 tablespoons chilled unsalted butter, cut into ½-inch cubes

½ cup iced water, plus more if necessary

1 quart Apple-Pear Meatless Mincemeat (page 194)

1 egg yolk

1 tablespoon milk

4. Roll out the smaller disk to a 12-inch circle about ⅛ inch thick. Center the dough over the top of the pie. Press the edges of the two circles of dough together to seal. Trim off the overhanging top circle of dough, leaving a 1-inch border around the edge of the pan. Roll up the dough border into a rope and flute. Cut a small hole in the center of the top crust.

5. In a small bowl, beat the egg yolk and milk until combined. Lightly brush the top of the pie with some of the yolk mixture. If desired, cut out designs from the excess dough and place on the glazed top crust. Lightly brush the cutouts with the beaten yolk mixture. Place the pie on a baking sheet.

6. Bake for 10 minutes. Reduce the oven temperature to 375°F and continue baking until the pie is golden brown and you can see the mincemeat bubbling through the center hole, 30 to 40 minutes. If the crust begins to brown too deeply, cover the pie loosely with aluminum foil.

7. Serve warm or at room temperature.

Pear and Hazelnut Brown Betty

In this slow-cooked version, pears are layered with spices and bread cubes, with the bread soaking up all of the delicious juices.

1. In a small bowl, combine the sugar, cinnamon, allspice, and cloves.

2. Place one third of the bread cubes in a 3½-quart slow cooker. Add half the pears, then sprinkle with half the sugar mixture and one third of the butter cubes. Layer with the remaining pears and sugar mixture, and half the remaining butter. Top with the remaining bread cubes and sprinkle with the remaining butter.

3. Cover and slow-cook until the pears are tender, about 2½ hours on high (300°F). Sprinkle with the nuts.

4. Serve hot or warm, topping each serving with a dollop of whipped cream.

Toasting nuts brings out their flavor. Spread the nuts in a single layer on a baking sheet. Bake, stirring once or twice, in a preheated 350°F oven until fragrant and lightly toasted, 10 to 15 minutes.

To skin toasted hazelnuts, wrap in a clean kitchen towel. Let the nuts stand 15 minutes, then use the towel to rub the skins off. (Some of the peel will remain on the hazelnuts no matter how hard you try.)

½ cup sugar

½ teaspoon ground cinnamon

½ teaspoon ground allspice

⅛ teaspoon ground cloves

9 slices firm-textured bread, cut into ½-inch cubes

2 pounds Bosc pears (about 4 medium pears), peeled, cored, and cut into 1-inch cubes

6 tablespoons unsalted butter, cut into ½-inch cubes

½ cup hazelnuts, toasted, skinned, and coarsely chopped (about 2 ounces)

Sweetened whipped cream, for garnish

Honeyed Apple-Orange Pudding

Another scrumptious recipe from Grandma Edith's files that works beautifully in the slow cooker. The "pudding" separates into three distinct layers: a honey and orange sauce, a cinnamon-scented sweet biscuit, and a chopped apple and nut topping. I serve it warm with a dab of sweetened sour cream. Select firm, tart apples that hold their shape during cooking, such as Granny Smith, Baldwin, Pippin, or Empire.

Makes 4 to 6 servings

1 cup all-purpose flour

1/3 cup plus 2 tablespoons sugar, divided

1 1/2 teaspoons baking powder

1/2 teaspoon salt

4 tablespoons cold unsalted butter, cut into 1/2-inch cubes

1/2 cup milk

1 medium tart apple, such as Granny Smith, peeled, cored, and cut into 1/2-inch cubes

1/4 cup coarsely chopped walnuts (about 1 ounce)

3/4 cup orange juice

1/4 cup honey

1 tablespoon unsalted butter, melted

1/2 teaspoon ground cinnamon

2/3 cup sour cream

2 tablespoons confectioners' sugar

1. In a medium bowl, whisk the flour, the 1/3 cup sugar, the baking powder, and salt to combine. Using a pastry blender or two knives, cut in the cold butter until the mixture resembles coarse meal. Stir in the milk to make a stiff dough. Spread the dough evenly over the bottom of a lightly buttered 3 1/2-quart slow cooker. Sprinkle the chopped apple and walnuts over the dough.

2. In a medium bowl, whisk the orange juice, honey, remaining 2 tablespoons sugar, the melted butter, and cinnamon until combined. Pour over the apples and walnuts.

3. Cover and cook until the apples are tender, 2 hours on high (300°F). (Do not cook on low for a longer period of time.)

4. In a small bowl, whisk the sour cream and confectioners' sugar until combined.

5. Spoon the warm pudding into individual bowls, and top each serving with a dollop of the sweetened sour cream.

Figgy Pudding Noël

This famous dish uses bread crumbs as its main ingredient, so it follows that your pudding will only be as good as your crumbs. Buy the firmest, least-sweet sandwich bread available (such as Pepperidge Farm). Lay it out in rows, let stand at room temperature overnight to become stale, then pulverize into crumbs in a food processor or blender. (Do *not* use packaged dried bread crumbs.)

Makes 6 to 8 servings

1. Generously butter the inside of a 2½-quart fluted tube pudding mold. Dust the inside of the mold with flour, and tap out the excess.

2. In a medium bowl, moisten the bread crumbs with the milk. In another bowl, combine the figs and Cognac. Let both mixtures stand, stirring occasionally, for 10 minutes.

3. In a large bowl, whisk the eggs, sugar, melted butter, baking powder, and salt until combined. Whisk in the soaked crumbs and the figs, with the Cognac. Pour the batter into the prepared mold. Cover with its lid or foil. Place in a 5-quart slow cooker and pour 3 cups hot water around the mold.

4. Cover and slow-cook until a toothpick inserted in the center of the pudding comes out clean, about 2½ hours on high (300°F). (Do not cook on low for a longer period of time.) Let the pudding stand for 5 minutes before unmolding.

5. Unmold the pudding onto a platter. Slice and serve warm, topped with a dollop of whipped cream.

2½ cups fine, dry, freshly ground bread crumbs (made from about 12 slices stale bread, crusts trimmed off)

½ cup milk

1 cup finely chopped figs (about 8 ounces), preferably Calimyrna

3 tablespoons Cognac, brandy, or apple juice

3 large eggs, at room temperature

1 cup sugar

4 tablespoons unsalted butter, melted

1½ teaspoons baking powder

½ teaspoon salt

Sweetened whipped cream, for garnish

Poached Pears with Mulled Wine Sauce

This dessert can be made a day or so ahead of time, making it even more appealing. Use Bosc pears, as their texture holds up to prolonged cooking.

Makes 4 servings

1. Using a vegetable peeler, peel the pears. Rub the pears with the lemon to prevent discoloration. Trim the bottom of each pear so it will stand upright.

2. In a 3½-quart slow cooker, combine the red wine, brown sugar, cinnamon stick, orange zest, allspice berries, and cloves. Stir to dissolve the sugar. Arrange the pears in a circle in the slow cooker, tilting them on their sides to submerge as much as possible in the red wine syrup. Cover and slow-cook until the pears are tender when pierced with the tip of a sharp knife, 5 to 6 hours on low (200°F) or 2½ to 3 hours on high (300°F).

3. Using a slotted spoon, carefully transfer the pears to a medium bowl. Strain the red wine syrup into a small saucepan. Cook the syrup over high heat until reduced to 1 cup, about 10 minutes. Pour the syrup over the pears. Cool to room temperature. (The pears and syrup can be prepared up to 2 days ahead, covered, and refrigerated. Return to room temperature before serving.)

4. To serve, place a pear in the center of each dessert plate. Pour the syrup around the pears and serve immediately.

4 medium Bosc pears (about 1½ pounds)

1 lemon, halved

2 cups dry red wine, such as Zinfandel

¾ cup packed light brown sugar

1 3-inch cinnamon stick

Zest of 1 small orange (removed with a vegetable peeler)

1 teaspoon whole allspice berries

6 whole cloves

Crème Caramel Valencia

This recipe guarantees a luscious crème caramel, a golden disk of custard swimming in a caramel sauce. All of the bugaboos of oven-baked custards (a tough "skin" topping, watery texture, curdling) disappear when you use the gentle heat of the slow cooker.

Makes 4 servings

1 cup sugar, divided

2 tablespoons water

2 cups milk

2 medium oranges, zest removed with a vegetable peeler and reserved

1 3-inch cinnamon stick

3 large eggs, at room temperature

1 teaspoon vanilla extract

1. In a small saucepan over medium heat, bring ½ cup of the sugar and the water to a boil, stirring constantly to help dissolve the sugar. As soon as the mixture boils, stop stirring and cook, occasionally swirling the pot by the handle, until the syrup has turned a deep golden brown, about 4 minutes. Immediately pour the syrup into a 1-quart soufflé dish. Using pot holders to protect your hands, quickly tilt the dish to coat the bottom and sides with the syrup, and set aside.

2. In a medium, heavy-bottomed saucepan, combine the milk, orange zest, and cinnamon stick and bring to a low simmer over medium heat. Remove from the heat, cover, and let stand for at least 10 minutes. Discard the zest and cinnamon stick.

3. In a medium bowl, whisk together the remaining ½ cup sugar, the eggs, and vanilla. Gradually whisk in the flavored milk. Pour into the prepared dish. Cover the dish with foil.

4. Place a collapsible vegetable steamer or a trivet in the bottom of a 5-quart slow cooker. Pour in 2 cups of hot water. Set the soufflé dish on the steamer or trivet, cover, and slow-cook until a knife inserted in the center of the custard comes out clean, about 2½ hours. Let the dish stand in the slow cooker until cool enough to remove.

5. Refrigerate, covered, until firm, at least 3 hours, or overnight.

6. Using a serrated knife, cut the rind off the oranges. Slice the oranges crosswise into ½-inch-thick rounds. Cover and refrigerate the orange rounds until serving time.

7. To unmold the custard, run a sharp knife around the inside of the dish. Dip the bottom of the dish into a large bowl of hot water for 15 seconds. Place a large plate on top of the dish. Hold the plate and dish together and invert them, giving a firm shake to release the custard and sauce onto the plate. Serve the custard, sliced into wedges, with the caramel sauce and the orange rounds.

Stuffed Apples with Maple-Rum Butterscotch

When making these tender apples with their luscious caramel sauce, be sure to choose a variety of apple that holds its shape during cooking, such as Rome, Granny Smith, or Cortland. While these raisin-and-nut-stuffed apples make a welcome dessert to finish an autumnal dinner, they can also be served for brunch with sautéed ham slices.

Serves 4

1. Stir the lemon juice into a medium bowl of cold water. Using a vegetable peeler, remove the peel from the top third of one of the apples. Using the end of the vegetable peeler, remove and discard the core and seeds from the apple, digging a channel ¾ to 1-inch wide that stops about ¼ inch from the bottom of the apple. Drop the apple into the lemon water. Repeat the procedure with the remaining apples.

2. In a small bowl, mix the 1 tablespoon brown sugar, the raisins, pecans, and 1 tablespoon of the butter with your fingers until combined. Drain the apples, and stuff with the raisin mixture.

3. In a 3½-quart slow cooker, combine the syrup, cinnamon stick, and the remaining ¼ cup brown sugar and 2 tablespoons butter. Stack the apples in the slow cooker. (They don't have to fit in a single layer.) Cover and slow-cook until the apples are tender

Juice of 1 lemon

4 large apples, preferably Rome, Granny Smith, or Cortland

¼ cup plus 1 tablespoon light brown sugar, divided

¼ cup dark raisins

¼ cup coarsely chopped pecans

3 tablespoons unsalted butter, divided

½ cup pancake syrup or pure maple syrup

1 cinnamon stick

1 tablespoon dark rum, bourbon, or Cognac

when pierced with the tip of a sharp knife, 3 to 4 hours on low (200°F) or 1½ to 2 hours on high (300°F).

4. Using a slotted spoon, carefully transfer the apples to four bowls. Cover with foil to keep warm.

5. Pour the syrup into a medium saucepan and boil over medium-high heat until thickened and reduced to about ½ cup. Stir in the rum. Drizzle the sauce over the apples and serve hot, warm, or at room temperature.

Variation: *To gild the lily, serve with scoops of vanilla ice cream or frozen yogurt.*

Pure maple syrup has an elusive flavor that may be lost during long cooking. It's expensive, too, and is probably at its best simply poured over pancakes. For the strongest maple flavor in this dessert, use supermarket variety pancake syrup.

Cranberry-Citrus Cake with Lemon Cream

Another festive tube cake, this one with the refreshing tanginess of cranberries, orange, lemon, and sour cream. (Don't forget to grate the zest from the oranges and lemons first before squeezing the juices.)

Makes 6 to 8 servings

1. *For the lemon cream:* In a chilled medium bowl, using a hand-held electric mixer set at high speed, beat the cream, sour cream, confectioners' sugar, and lemon zest just until soft peaks begin to form. Cover and refrigerate until chilled, or up to 4 hours.

2. *For the cake:* Generously butter the inside of a 2½-quart fluted tube pudding mold. Dust the inside of the mold with flour, and tap out the excess.

3. In a medium bowl, using a hand-held electric mixer set at medium-high speed, beat the butter until creamy. Add the sugar and beat until light in color and texture, about 2 minutes. Beat in the eggs, one at a time. Beat in the vanilla and orange zest.

4. Sift the flour, baking powder, and salt together onto a piece of waxed paper. Beat the flour mixture and the milk, alternately in thirds, into the butter-sugar mixture, scraping down the sides of the bowl with a rubber spatula. (The batter will be thick.) Stir in the cranberries and walnuts. Transfer to the prepared mold and cover with its lid or foil.

LEMON CREAM

¾ cup heavy cream

¼ cup sour cream

2 tablespoons confectioners' sugar

Grated zest of 1 lemon

CRANBERRY-CITRUS CAKE

6 tablespoons unsalted butter, softened

¾ cup sugar

2 large eggs, at room temperature

1 teaspoon vanilla extract

Grated zest of 1 orange

2¼ cups all-purpose flour

2½ teaspoons baking powder

¼ teaspoon salt

½ cup milk

5. Place the mold in a 5-quart slow cooker and pour 2 cups hot water around the mold. Cover and slow-cook until a cake tester inserted in the center of the cake comes out clean, 2½ to 3 hours on high (300°F). (Do not cook on low for a longer period of time.)

6. Meanwhile, in a small bowl, whisk the orange and lemon juices with the confectioners' sugar to dissolve the sugar.

7. Pour half the orange juice mixture over the hot cake; let stand for 5 minutes. Unmold the cake onto a serving platter. Drizzle the remaining juice mixture over the top of the cake, and let stand 5 minutes longer. Serve warm or at room temperature with the Lemon Cream.

2 cups fresh cranberries (8 ounces), rinsed and picked over

½ cup coarsely chopped toasted walnuts

⅓ cup fresh orange juice

2 tablespoons fresh lemon juice

⅓ cup confectioners' sugar

Pumpkin Crème Brûlée

Makes 4 servings

1 15-ounce can pumpkin purée
1¼ cups sugar, divided
1 teaspoon ground cinnamon
½ teaspoon ground ginger
½ teaspoon ground nutmeg
3 large eggs, at room temperature
1 cup heavy cream, scalded
2 tablespoons water
⅛ teaspoon cream of tartar dissolved in 1 teaspoon water

1. In a medium bowl, whisk together the pumpkin, ¾ cup of the sugar, the cinnamon, ginger, and nutmeg. Add the eggs and whisk until smooth. Gradually whisk in the scalded heavy cream. Pour into a 1-quart soufflé dish. Cover tightly with aluminum foil.

2. Place a collapsible vegetable steamer or slow-cooker meat rack in the bottom of a 5-quart slow cooker. Place the soufflé dish on the steamer or rack. Add enough hot water to come 1 inch up the side of the dish. Cover and slow-cook until a knife inserted in the center of the custard comes out clean, about 3 hours on high (300°F). (Do not cook on low for a longer period of time.) Let the dish stand in the slow cooker until cool enough to remove.

3. Refrigerate the custard, covered, until very cold, at least 6 hours, or overnight.

4. In a small saucepan over medium heat, bring the remaining ½ cup sugar and the water to a boil, stirring constantly to help dissolve the sugar. As soon as the mixture starts boiling, add the cream of tartar mixture. Stop stirring and cook, occasionally swirling the pot by the handle, until the syrup has turned a deep golden brown, about 4 minutes. Immediately, and carefully, pour the syrup over the surface of the pumpkin custard, tilting the dish so the caramel evenly coats the surface. Let stand until the caramel has hardened, about 5 minutes. (The crème brûlée can be prepared 1 day ahead, covered, and refrigerated.)

Beverages and Punches

A hot beverage is an effective way of chasing away the winter blahs. Hot brews are always popular at large celebrations, especially during the holiday season, but I serve them at smaller get-togethers, too. After-ski gatherings, winter brunches, and Super Bowl parties are just a few opportunities to turn your slow cooker into a punch bowl.

The slow cooker is absolutely the best appliance to prepare hot punches and beverages for three reasons: The long brewing period allows the spices to steep into the drink without scorching; the beverages are served directly from the slow cooker, making for easy preparation and cleanup; and the slow cooker keeps the drinks at perfect serving temperature for hours.

I like to "spike" my hot punches, but if you prefer, serve the liquor on the side, allowing each guest to add spirits to taste.

Steve's Scandinavian Apple-Berry Punch

This crowd-pleasing hot punch comes from a friend, Manhattan caterer Steve Austin, and it is a staple at Austin and Company's holiday gatherings. The lingonberry juice (available at specialty grocers and Scandinavian markets) makes it special, but cranberry juice can stand in. The spices are slowly steeped in the juice in the slow cooker, giving the fullest measure of their flavor. The rum is optional, and can be served on the side for each guest to spike his or her punch at will.

Makes 12 to 16 servings

1½ teaspoons whole allspice berries

1½ teaspoons whole cloves

1 3-inch cinnamon stick

2 quarts freshly squeezed apple cider

1 quart lingonberry or cranberry juice

1 tablespoon aromatic bitters

1 orange, cut into thick slices

1 cup dark rum

Cinnamon sticks, for garnish

1. Wrap the allspice, cloves, and cinnamon stick in a rinsed and squeezed-dry piece of cheesecloth, and tie with a piece of kitchen string.

2. In a 3½-quart slow cooker, combine the spice packet with the apple cider, lingonberry juice, bitters, and orange slices.

3. Cover and slow-cook until the mixture is very hot, but not boiling, about 4 hours on low (200°F) or 2 hours on high (300°F). Remove the spice packet and stir in the rum.

4. Turn the heat to low (200°F). The slow cooker will keep the punch at serving temperature for at least 4 hours. Serve the punch in punch glasses or mugs, garnished with cinnamon sticks.

In any cooking, use dark rum for the best, most intense flavor.

Carolers' Mulled Wine

Frankly, mulled wine used to remind me of bad Christmas parties, where the drink had been boiling for what seemed like days to form a bitter brew. Now that I make mulled wine in the slow cooker, where it is gently warmed, not boiled, I have happier thoughts on this holiday classic. I accent the orange flavor with a healthy dose of Grand Marnier.

Makes 12 servings

1 *large orange*

12 *whole cloves*

2 *3-inch cinnamon sticks*

3 *cardamom pods, crushed*

2 *bottles dry red wine, such as Zinfandel*

1 *cup honey*

2/3 *cup Grand Marnier or other orange-flavored liqueur*

1. Stud the orange with the cloves. Wrap the cinnamon sticks and cardamom seeds in a rinsed and squeezed-dry piece of cheesecloth, and tie with a piece of kitchen twine.

2. In a 3½-quart slow cooker, combine the wine, honey, studded orange, and spice packet. Cover and slow-cook until hot, about 4 hours on low (200°F). (Do not cook the mixture on high for a shorter period of time, unless you are careful not to let the mixture come to a boil.)

3. Just before serving, discard the spice packet and stir the Grand Marnier into the wine. The slow cooker will keep the punch at proper serving temperature for at least 4 hours.

Wassail

Not every hot, mulled punch is a "wassail." True wassail (from the term *was hale,* Old Anglo-Saxon for "be hearty") is made from ale and sherry and garnished with roasted apples. The Anglo-Saxons had plenty of home-brewed ale, and they got their sherry from nearby Spain. Wassail was originally garnished with toast (giving us the phrase "drink a toast") and eggs, but I think modern tastes will prefer this streamlined version.

Makes 12 servings

1.   Preheat the oven to 350°F.

2.   Using a vegetable peeler, remove the peel from the top third of each apple. Cut each apple into 6 wedges, and trim out the core. Stud each wedge with a clove and place on a baking sheet. Bake the apples until just tender, about 25 minutes. Set the apple wedges aside.

3.   Wrap the cloves, ginger, allspice, and cinnamon sticks in a piece of rinsed and squeezed-dry cheesecloth, and tie with a piece of kitchen twine.

4.   In a 3½-quart slow cooker, combine the ale, sherry, brown sugar, spice packet, and lemon slices. Cover and slow-cook until very hot, about 4 hours on low (200°F). (Do not cook the mixture on high for a shorter period of time, unless you are careful not to let it come to a boil.)

2 large Rome or Granny Smith apples

12 whole cloves

2 tablespoons chopped crystallized ginger

12 whole allspice berries

2 3-inch cinnamon sticks

3 12-ounce bottles ale

2 cups semisweet sherry, such as Oloroso

¼ cup packed light brown sugar

1 medium lemon, sliced into ¼-inch-thick rounds

5. Just before serving, discard the spice packet and add the reserved roasted apples to the wassail. Serve in punch glasses, and if you serve a piece of the roasted apple in each glass, so much the better. The slow cooker will keep the wassail at the proper serving temperature for at least 4 hours.

Grand Hot Chocolate Punch

I can't think of anything that would be better to come back to after a cold afternoon of skiing. Nonfat milk instead of regular keeps the mixture from separating.

Makes 8 servings

1. In a 3½-quart slow cooker, whisk the milk powder, sugar, and cocoa powder until combined. Gradually whisk in the water, then add the orange zest and cinnamon sticks. Cover and slow-cook until very hot, 4 to 5 hours on low (200°F).

2. Remove and discard the zest and cinnamon sticks. Whisk the punch until smooth. Stir in the brandy. Serve the punch in mugs, topped with whipped cream. (If the punch thickens upon standing, whisk again.)

4 3.2-ounce envelopes nonfat dry milk powder (about 4 cups)

¾ cup sugar

¾ cup unsweetened cocoa powder

2 quarts water

Zest of 1 orange (removed with a vegetable peeler)

2 3-inch cinnamon sticks

½ cup brandy or dark rum (optional)

Lightly sweetened whipped cream, for garnish

Steamy Mary

This tomato-beef-broth-and-vodka sipper is a convivial addition to a winter brunch menu or an after-ski get-together. Add the vodka, horseradish, and hot red pepper sauce just before serving, as they will lose their impact if heated too long.

Makes 6 to 8 servings

1. In a 3½-quart slow cooker, combine the tomato-and-vegetable juice, beef broth, water, and celery seeds. Cover and slow-cook until very hot, about 4 hours on low (200°F).

2. Just before serving, stir in the vodka, horseradish, and red pepper sauce. Ladle into mugs or punch glasses, garnishing each serving with a celery stick and a lime wedge.

1½ quarts tomato-and-vegetable juice (such as V-8)

1⅓ cups double-strength beef broth

1 cup water

2 teaspoons celery seeds

¾ cup vodka

2 tablespoons prepared horseradish

½ teaspoon hot red pepper sauce

Celery sticks, for garnish

Lime wedges, for garnish

Apricot Glow Punch

Tea lovers will go for this golden, warming punch with a splash of Cognac.

Makes 8 to 12 servings

1. In a large heatproof pitcher, steep the tea in the water for 10 minutes.

2. Strain into a 3½-quart slow cooker. Stir in the apricot nectar, ginger, and cinnamon sticks. Cover and slow-cook until hot, about 4 hours on low (200°F).

3. Just before serving, stir in the Cognac. The slow cooker will keep the punch at serving temperature for up to 3 hours.

¼ cup loose Orange Pekoe tea

1 quart boiling water

1 46-ounce can apricot nectar

6 ¼-inch-thick slices fresh ginger

2 3-inch cinnamon sticks

½ cup Cognac or brandy

Go-Withs

With the main course simmering away on its own in the slow cooker, you'll have extra time to prepare accompaniments to the meal on the stove or in the oven. Here's a collection of easy-to-make go-withs that you'll find complementary to your soups, stews, or ragoûts.

Quick breads differ from yeast breads in that they use baking soda or baking powder for leavening. They are faster to prepare because you don't have to wait for the bread to rise before baking. (In fact, do not delay in putting the quick breads in the oven, or the batter may deflate.) Sour Cream Corn Bread is sensational with any of the slow-cooked chilis. Serve Down-Home Collard Greens (page 176) in a bowl with a good helping of its pot liquor and a hunk of the corn bread for a Southern luncheon. Irish Currant Soda Bread and Oatmeal Raisin Muffins can be served with any of the soups and stews, since they have only a hint of sweetness. Best-Ever Buttermilk Biscuits are welcome with any main course, but are particularly well-suited to Chicken and Root Vegetable Fricassee (page 149). If you'd like to prepare a yeast bread with a minimum of time and effort, the Garlic and Rosemary Focaccia is for you.

Most of the slow-cooked main dishes are served with a sauce or gravy. These sauces are best appreciated with a starchy side dish to soak up every last drop of goodness. Garlic Mashed Potatoes are an upscale version of mashed potatoes that are great with Bollito Misto (page 92) or

Sweet and Sour Beef Brisket (page 131). When you want a potato dish with crunch, serve a Giant Potato Cake, the perfect match for ragoûts like Harvesttime Pork and Apple Stew (page 99). Any of the curries would go well with Herbed Rice, and the saffron variation is made for Osso Buco (page 107).

Hearty slow-cooked soups, stews, chilis, or pot roasts often need nothing more but a salad and bread to make a full meal. I offer two of my favorite salads to round out your menu. Chinese Cabbage and Peanut Slaw would be nice with the Oriental flavors of Chinese Chicken Hot Pot (page 40) or Chinese Country Ribs (page 104). Mixed Greens Salad with Cheddar and Apples is a winner with just about any main course, but I like it best with The Pot Roast (page 124).

Sour Cream Corn Bread

This moist, melt-in-your-mouth corn bread is almost more like a not-too-sweet cake than a bread. It's the sour cream that gives it such a tender crumb.

Makes 6 to 8 servings

1. Position a rack in the top third of the oven and preheat the oven to 425°F. Lightly oil an 8-inch round cake pan, and place the pan in the oven to heat for 3 minutes.

2. In a large bowl, whisk the cornmeal, flour, sugar, baking powder, baking soda, and salt to combine. In a small bowl, whisk the sour cream and eggs until well combined. Stir into the flour mixture until just mixed.

3. Spread the batter in the hot pan. Bake until a toothpick inserted in the center of the bread comes out clean, 20 to 25 minutes. Serve hot or warm.

Chile and Cheddar Corn Bread: *Stir 1 seeded and minced hot fresh chile pepper (such as jalapeño) into the batter with the sour cream. Pour into the prepared pan, then sprinkle ½ cup shredded sharp Cheddar cheese on top. Bake as directed.*

1 cup yellow cornmeal, preferably stone-ground

1 cup all-purpose flour

1 tablespoon sugar

2 teaspoons baking powder

½ teaspoon baking soda

½ teaspoon salt

1 cup sour cream

2 large eggs

Brahmin Brown Bread

My dictionary says that "Brahmin" refers to "a member of a New England family that is considered aristocratic." Surely brown bread—slightly sweet with a harmonious blend of grains and molasses—is the aristocrat of Yankee breads. Since it is always steamed, rather than baked, it is a fine bread to prepare in the slow cooker. Serve it warm, with sweet butter, at any meal. It is traditionally prepared in a coffee can, but I prefer a steamed pudding mold (see page 187).

Makes 1 loaf (6 to 8 slices)

1 cup milk

1 tablespoon lemon juice or cider vinegar

1 cup all-purpose flour

1 cup rye flour

1 cup yellow cornmeal

2 teaspoons baking soda

1 teaspoon salt

6 tablespoons molasses

2 tablespoons unsalted butter, melted

1/2 cup dark raisins

1. Lightly butter the inside of a 2 1/2-quart fluted tube pudding mold. Dust the inside of the mold with flour and tap out the excess.

2. In a glass measuring cup, combine the milk and lemon juice. Let stand until the milk is soured and slightly clabbered, about 10 minutes.

3. In a large bowl, whisk both flours, the cornmeal, baking soda, and salt to combine. Add the soured milk, molasses, and melted butter and whisk just until smooth. Stir in the raisins. Pour into the prepared mold.

4. Cover the mold with its lid or a double thickness of aluminum foil. Place in a 5-quart slow cooker and pour 3 cups of hot water around the mold. Cover and slow-cook until a toothpick inserted in the center of the bread comes out clean, about 3 hours on high (300°F). (Do not cook on low for a longer period of time.)

5. Unmold the bread and let stand for 5 minutes before slicing. Serve while still warm.

Irish Currant Soda Bread

To complete your St. Patrick's Day feast, serve this bread with a slow-cooked Yankee Corned Beef with Maple-Mustard Glaze and Winter Vegetables (page 142). But because it can be made in a snap, I like to serve this year-round as a breakfast treat, spread with Gingered Apple Butter (page 183).

Make 1 loaf, about 8 servings

1. Position a rack in the top third of the oven and preheat the oven to 375°F.

2. In a large bowl, whisk the flour, baking powder, baking soda, and salt to combine. Add the currants and caraway seeds and mix well. In a medium bowl, whisk the buttermilk, melted butter, honey, and egg until combined. Stir into the flour mixture and mix just until combined. Knead the mixture in the bowl for about 1 minute, adding more flour if necessary, to form a soft dough.

3. Form the dough into a large ball about 5½ inches in diameter, and place on an ungreased baking sheet. Using a sharp knife, cut a large cross, about ¼ inch deep, in the top of the dough.

4. Bake until the bread is golden brown and sounds hollow when tapped on the bottom, 45 to 55 minutes. Transfer to a wire cake rack and cool completely.

Variation: *Use chopped dried apples, pears, or apricots instead of the currants or raisins. Dried blueberries or cranberries, available at specialty grocers, make excellent, if pricey, additions.*

2½ cups all-purpose flour, plus more if needed

1½ teaspoons baking powder

½ teaspoon baking soda

½ teaspoon salt

½ cup dried currants or dark raisins

1½ teaspoons caraway seeds (optional)

¾ cup buttermilk

4 tablespoons unsalted butter, melted

2 tablespoons honey

1 large egg

If you don't have buttermilk on hand, try this substitution: For each cup of buttermilk needed, mix 2 teaspoons cider vinegar or lemon juice into 1 cup whole or low-fat milk and let stand until clabbered, 10 to 15 minutes.

Oatmeal Raisin Muffins

Chewy with oats and raisins, and only slightly sweet, these healthy treats can be served, hot out of the oven, for breakfast, lunch, or dinner.

Makes 1 dozen

1. Position a rack in the top third of the oven and preheat the oven to 400°F. Lightly butter the insides of 12 muffin cups.

2. In a large bowl, whisk the flour, oatmeal, brown sugar, baking powder, and salt to combine. Add the raisins and mix well. In a small bowl, whisk the milk, oil, and eggs until combined. Stir into the flour mixture, just until combined. Do not overmix the batter.

3. Spoon the batter into the prepared cups, filling each about two thirds full. Bake until a toothpick inserted in the center of a muffin comes out clean, about 20 minutes. Serve hot.

1⅓ cups all-purpose flour

1⅓ cups quick-cooking oatmeal (not "instant")

⅓ cup packed light brown sugar, rubbed through a sieve to remove lumps

2½ teaspoons baking powder

1¼ teaspoons salt

⅔ cup dark raisins

1⅓ cups milk

¼ cup vegetable oil

2 large eggs

Best-Ever Buttermilk Biscuits

A combination of cake and all-purpose flour gives these tender, flaky biscuits their light-as-a-feather goodness. Biscuits are always best when served as soon as they're done, spread with as much butter as you dare.

Makes 1 dozen

1. Position a rack in the center of the oven and preheat the oven to 400°F.

2. In a large bowl, whisk the cake flour, all-purpose flour, cream of tartar, baking soda, and salt to combine. Using a pastry blender or two knives, cut in the butter until the mixture resembles coarse meal. Mix in the buttermilk just until combined. Knead the dough lightly in the bowl, just to form a soft dough. Do not overwork.

3. On a lightly floured surface, pat out the dough with floured hands to a ¾-inch thickness. Using a 2½-inch round cookie cutter or a glass, cut out biscuits. Gather up the scraps, pat out again, and cut out more biscuits to get a total of 12. Place the biscuits on an ungreased baking sheet.

4. Bake until the biscuits are risen and golden brown, 12 to 15 minutes. Serve hot.

Herb Biscuits: *Stir ¼ cup chopped fresh chives, basil, parsley, or dill into the buttermilk before adding to the dough.*

Ginger Biscuits: *Stir ¼ cup minced crystallized ginger into the flour mixture.*

1½ cups cake flour (not self-rising)

1½ cups bleached all-purpose flour

1 tablespoon cream of tartar

1½ teaspoons baking soda

¾ teaspoon salt

12 tablespoons (1½ sticks) unsalted butter, cut into ½-inch cubes

1 cup plus 2 tablespoons buttermilk

Chinese Cabbage and Peanut Slaw

For an Oriental salad to accompany Chinese-inspired dishes, here's a quick, unusual slaw that is even better if made ahead. Chinese cabbage (also called "Napa" or "nappa") is a tender, mildly flavored, pale green cabbage. Even greengrocers sometimes confuse it with bok choy, which is dark green with white stalks, so don't make that mistake.

Makes 4 to 6 servings

1. In a large bowl, whisk together the vinegar, sugar, salt, and pepper. Gradually whisk in the oil until combined. Add the cabbage, carrots, and scallions and toss well. (The slaw can be prepared up to 1 day ahead, covered, and refrigerated.)

2. Just before serving, stir in the peanuts.

6 tablespoons rice or white vinegar

1 teaspoon sugar

1/2 teaspoon salt

1/4 teaspoon freshly ground black pepper

3/4 cup peanut or vegetable oil

1 small head Chinese cabbage (about 1 1/4 pounds), cored and cut crosswise into 1/4-inch-wide shreds

2 medium carrots, grated

2 scallions, finely chopped

1/2 cup unsalted peanuts, coarsely chopped

Garlic and Rosemary Focaccia

Makes 6 to 8 servings

1. Pour the lukewarm water into a small bowl, and stir in the yeast and sugar. Let stand until foamy, about 10 minutes. Stir to dissolve the yeast, then stir in the remaining ¾ cup water and 2 tablespoons of the oil.

2. In a food processor fitted with the metal blade, combine the flour and salt and pulse to mix. With the machine running, pour in the yeast mixture. Process until the dough forms a ball on top of the blade. If the dough is too wet or too dry, it will not form a ball: Feel the dough, and if it is sticky and wet, add additional flour, 2 tablespoons at a time, and process until the dough forms a ball. If the dough is crumbly and dry, add 1 tablespoon of water at a time, and process until the dough forms a ball. Process the ball for 45 seconds to knead into a smooth, elastic dough.

3. Place the ball of dough in a lightly oiled bowl, turn to coat with the oil, and cover with plastic wrap. Let stand in a warm, draft-free place until doubled in bulk, about 1 hour.

4. Position two racks in the bottom third and in the center of the oven and preheat the oven to 400°F.

5. Divide the dough in half, and roll out two 10-inch circles. Place the circles on two baking sheets. Press the chopped rosemary and garlic slivers into the tops of the dough. Drizzle each round with 1½ teaspoons of the remaining oil, then sprinkle with the

¼ cup lukewarm (100 to 110°F) water plus ¾ cup tap water

1 package dry active yeast

¼ teaspoon granulated sugar

3 tablespoons extra-virgin olive oil, divided

3 cups unbleached all-purpose flour, plus more if needed

1 teaspoon salt

2 tablespoons chopped fresh rosemary

2 garlic cloves, cut into slivers

½ teaspoon coarse (kosher) salt, for sprinkling

coarse salt. Bake until golden brown, switching the positions of the baking sheets halfway through the baking time, about 15 minutes in all.

6. Serve hot, warm, or at room temperature.

Garlic and Olive Focaccia: *After the dough has been removed from the food processor, knead ½ cup pitted and chopped black or green Mediterranean olives into the dough.*

Sun-Dried Tomato Focaccia: *After the dough has been removed from the food processor, knead ½ cup chopped sun-dried tomatoes packed in oil, patted dry with paper towels, into the dough.*

Garlic and Sage Focaccia: *Substitute 2 tablespoons chopped fresh sage for the rosemary.*

To make the focaccia with dried herbs, substitute 2 teaspoons dried rosemary or sage for the fresh. Knead the herbs into the dough by hand.

Quick breads (those leavened with baking powder or baking soda) are best when made with bleached all-purpose flour. However, yeast breads, such as focaccia, are best with unbleached all-purpose flour. The unbleached flour has a higher proportion of gluten, the protein that gives dough strength, and makes a firmer yeast bread.

Mixed Greens Salad with Cheddar and Apples

Curls of Cheddar cheese, crisp apple slices, and walnut nuggets lift this salad from the everyday to the extra-special.

Makes 4 to 6 servings

1. In a small bowl, whisk together the vinegar, salt, and pepper. Gradually whisk in the oil.

2. In a large bowl, combine the lettuces, apples, and walnuts. Using a vegetable peeler or cheese planer, slice the Cheddar into curls, letting the curls fall over the salad.

3. Present the salad at the table, then add the dressing and toss well. Serve immediately.

⅓ cup sherry or balsamic vinegar

½ teaspoon salt

¼ teaspoon freshly ground black pepper

⅔ cup olive oil

1 small head red leaf lettuce, rinsed and torn into pieces

1 small head green leaf lettuce, rinsed and torn into pieces

2 Granny Smith apples, quartered, cored, and thinly sliced

½ cup walnuts, toasted (see page 202)

4 ounces sharp Cheddar cheese (in 1 piece)

Autumntime Applesauce

One of autumn's premiere sensory pleasures is the aroma of simmering applesauce. Two factors contribute to great applesauce: great apples and temperate cooking. With the combination of a farmers' market close to my kitchen, and my slow cooker, I can make world-class applesauce. It is a versatile ingredient, and need not be restricted to dessert, as my variation for Mint-Apple Sauce testifies.

3 pounds apples, preferably Cortland or Jonathan, peeled, cored, and quartered

1/2 cup sugar

2 tablespoons lemon juice

1 3-inch cinnamon stick

2 tablespoons unsalted butter

Makes about 1 quart

1. In a 3 1/2-quart slow cooker, combine the apples, sugar, lemon juice, and cinnamon stick. Cover and slow-cook on high (300°F) until the apples are very tender 3 to 4 hours.

2. Remove and discard the cinnamon stick. Add the butter and stir in, mashing the apples to your desired consistency.

Mint-Apple Sauce: *Combine 1 cup Autumntime Applesauce with 2 tablespoons chopped fresh mint. This is an excellent condiment for roast pork or lamb.*

Hot Apple Pie in a Glass: *Place 1 scoop of ice cream in a wine goblet and top with 1/2 cup of warm Autumntime Applesauce. Crumble 3 or 4 shortbread cookies (such as Pepperidge Farm Chessmen) over the applesauce and serve immediately.*

Herbed Rice

It only takes a couple of minutes to add onions and herbs to plain steamed rice, and what a difference it makes. I also use chicken broth to add an extra dimension to what can be an uninspiring side dish.

Makes 4 to 6 servings

1. In a medium saucepan, melt the butter over low heat. Add the onion and cook, covered, until softened, about 5 minutes.

2. Increase the heat to medium and add the rice. Cook, stirring often, until the rice turns opaque, about 2 minutes. Stir in the water, chicken broth, salt, thyme, pepper, and bay leaf. Bring to a boil, reduce the heat to low, and cook, covered, until the rice is tender, about 20 minutes.

3. Stir in the chopped herbs, and remove the bay leaf before serving.

Saffron Herbed Rice: *Add ¹/₂ teaspoon crushed saffron threads to the rice along with the liquids.*

1 tablespoon unsalted butter

1 medium onion, chopped

1¹/₂ cups converted long-grain rice

2¹/₃ cups water

1 cup double-strength chicken broth

¹/₄ teaspoon salt

¹/₄ teaspoon dried thyme

¹/₈ teaspoon freshly ground black pepper

1 bay leaf

2 tablespoons chopped fresh dill, basil, or parsley

Giant Potato Cake

Crisp on the outside with an almost creamy interior, this is one of my favorite dishes. I serve it most often as a side dish, cut into wedges, to go with stews. But who could resist it at breakfast time served with Autumntime Applesauce (page 231) and sour cream? While the potatoes and onion can be shredded on a hand grater, the food processor makes the shortest work of this chore. Use a nonstick skillet to be sure the potato cake can be flipped easily.

Makes 4 to 6 servings

3 large baking potatoes (such as Idaho or russet) (about 1½ pounds), peeled and shredded

1 medium onion, peeled and shredded

1 teaspoon salt

¼ teaspoon freshly ground black pepper

2 tablespoons vegetable oil

1 tablespoon unsalted butter

1. In a large bowl, toss the potatoes, onion, salt, and pepper. Let stand for 5 minutes. By handfuls, squeeze as much moisture as you can from the mixture.

2. In a medium nonstick skillet, heat the oil and butter over medium-high heat. Add the potato mixture, and pat it out into an even layer. Reduce the heat to medium low, cover, and cook until the bottom of the cake is golden brown, about 7 minutes.

3. Hold a large dinner plate over the top of the skillet. Flip the skillet and the plate upside down so the potato cake falls onto the plate, then slide the potato cake back into the skillet. Continue cooking, uncovered, until the bottom is browned, about 5 minutes.

4. To serve, slide the potato cake onto a plate, and cut into wedges.

Garlic Mashed Potatoes

I can't recall when I started cooking carrots with my potatoes for mashing, but I like the added color to what can be a bland-looking, if delicious, dish. The large amount of garlic will dissipate during boiling.

Makes 4 to 6 servings

1. In a large saucepan of boiling salted water over medium heat, cook the potatoes, carrots, and garlic until the potatoes are tender, about 30 minutes. Drain well.

2. In a medium bowl, using a hand-held electric mixer or a potato masher, mash the cooked vegetables with the butter, milk, salt, and pepper. Transfer to a warmed serving dish and serve immediately.

5 large baking potatoes (such as Idaho or russets) (about 2½ pounds), peeled and cut into 2-inch chunks

2 medium carrots, peeled and cut into 1-inch-long pieces

1 head garlic, separated into cloves and peeled

2 tablespoons unsalted butter

⅓ cup milk, heated

½ teaspoon salt

¼ teaspoon freshly ground white pepper

Index

Greek:
  stuffed artichokes with egg-lemon sauce, 164–165
  veal and baby onion stifado, 105
Green beans, Southern-style smothered, 177
Green peppers with turkey-corn, 161
Greens, mixed, salad with Cheddar and apples, 230
Ground beef chili with cornmeal dumplings, 53
Grunt, blueberry, 188
Guacamole salsa, 41
Gumbo, snapper, oyster, and ham, 68

H

Ham:
  Basque chicken and rice casserole, 155
  pink bean and pasta soup with, 51
  with port-raisin sauce, 135
  slow-cooked paella, 155
  snapper, and oyster gumbo, 68
  very nice red beans and rice, 74
Harvesttime pork and apple stew, 99
Hazelnut(s):
  and pear brown Betty, 202
  toasted, to skin, 202
Herb(ed):
  biscuits, 226
  rice, 232
  saffron rice, 232

sauce, Italian green, 93
Thanksgiving stuffing, 180–181
Herbs, fresh, cooking with, 37
Hester Street beef and rice cabbage rolls, 120–121
Hominy:
  pozole, 50
  and turkey chili, 58
Honeyed apple-orange pudding, 203
Hoppin' John, 78
Horseradish sauce, garden patch, short ribs with, 98
Hot fudge spooncake, 196
Huckleberry grunt, 188

I

Indonesian veal stew with coconut and peanuts, 106
Irish currant soda bread, 224–225
Italian:
  fonduto, 18
  green herb sauce, 93
  spinach and cheese timbale, 170–171

J

Jamaican oxtail soup, 49
Jambalaya, scallop, shrimp, and sausage, 70
Joy's Mexican pot roast, 128–129

K

Kale and sausage soup, Portuguese, 48

Karren's Bourbon Street bread pudding, 197

L

Lamb, 86–87
  black bean, sweet pepper, and goat cheese salad with, 85
  cassoulet, 80–81
  in chile rojo sauce, 110–111
  mushroom, and barley pilaf, 107
  and pine-nut–stuffed grape leaves, 20–21
  shanks in garlic sauce, 113
  shepherd's stew, 109
  split pea, and dill soup, 44
  stew with coconut and peanuts, Indonesian, 106
  vindaloo, 112
Lemon:
  cream, cranberry-citrus cake with, 210–211
  egg sauce, Greek stuffed artichokes with, 164–165
  raspberry pudding cake, 189
Lentil:
  and sausage stew, 75
  tomato stew, 75
Lingonberry-apple punch, Steve's Scandinavian, 214
Little Italy chicken cacciatore, 148
Liver, chicken, and apple terrine, 23
Lobster and corn chowder, farmers' market, 69
Louisiana yam and pineapple pudding, 178

P

Paella, slow-cooked, 155
Parmesan:
  Castroville artichoke dip, 15
  meatballs, spaghetti in herbed
    tomato sauce with, 116–
    117
  pistou, 37
  ravioli casserole, 115
  and spinach timbale, Italian,
    170–171
Pasta:
  Amish country chicken "pot
    pie," 147
  Athenian shrimp in tomato
    and feta sauce, 63
  beef Stroganoff, 94
  daube de boeuf, 90–91
  fennel pizzaiola, 169
  and pink bean soup with ham,
    51
  pot-au-feu, 130–131
  ravioli casserole, 115
  seafood etouffé, 64
  spaghetti in herbed tomato
    sauce with Parmesan
    meatballs, 116–117
Pâté, veal, pork, and spinach,
  22
Pea(s):
  salmon, and mushroom chow-
    der, 62
  shepherd's stew, 109
  slow-cooked paella, 155
  split, lamb, and dill soup, 44
Peanut(s):
  and Chinese cabbage slaw,
    227
  Indonesian veal stew with co-
    conut and, 106

sauce, spicy, chicken stew
  with, 158
Pear(s):
  apple meatless mincemeat,
    194
  cranberry-walnut sauce, 185
  and hazelnut brown Betty,
    202
  poached, with mulled wine
    sauce, 205
  soda bread, Irish, 224–225
Pecan(s):
  Cajun, 24
  chocolate pudding, steamed,
    198–199
  wild rice, and apricot dressing,
    182
Pepper(s):
  green, with turkey-corn, 161
  sweet, black bean, and goat
    cheese salad, 84–85
  see also Chile
Persimmon(s):
  gingerbread pudding,
    Grandma Edith's, 190–
    191
  varieties of, 191
Pickled vegetables, tarragon, 16
Pie, double-crust mincemeat,
  200–201
Pilaf, lamb, mushroom, and barley, 107
Pineapple:
  and macadamia chutney, 184–
    185
  and yam pudding, Louisiana,
    178
Pine nut(s):
  and lamb-stuffed grape leaves,
    20–21
  pistou, 36

Pink bean(s):
  frijoles gorditos, 76–77
  and pasta soup with ham,
    51
Pistou, 36
  Mediterranean vegetable soup
    with, 35
Poached pears with mulled wine
  sauce, 205
Pork, 86
  and apple stew, harvesttime,
    99
  bean, and cabbage soup,
    French, 52
  cassoulet, 80–81
  Chinese country ribs, 104
  hill country ribs, 104
  Joy's Mexican pot roast, 128–
    129
  loin in milk sauce, 137
  North Carolina rainy day
    "barbecued," 138
  old-fashioned meat loaf, 118–
    119
  port, and chestnut ragoût,
    100–101
  pozole, 50
  roast in orange sauce, 139
  roast with chile verde sauce,
    136
  and sausage cazuela, 102–103
  south of the border burritos,
    129
  stew with coconut and pea-
    nuts, Indonesian, 106
  veal, and spinach pâté, 22
  see also Ham
Portuguese:
  kale and sausage soup, 48
  spiced beef stew (soupas),
    95

Rosemary:
  and garlic focaccia, 228–229
  orangey beans, 73
Rum, 214
  maple butterscotch, stuffed
    apples with, 208–209
  Steve's Scandinavian apple-
    berry punch, 214

S

Saffron herbed rice, 232
Sage:
  and garlic focaccia, 229
  turkey breast saltimbocca, 160
  white beans with garlic and,
    79
Salad:
  black bean, sweet pepper, and
    goat cheese, 84–85
  caponata, 13
  Chinese cabbage and peanut
    slaw, 227
  mixed greens, with Cheddar
    and apples, 230
  orange-tarragon beet, 172
  ratatouille niçoise, 166–167
  white bean, tuna, and tomato,
    83
Salmon, mushroom, and pea
  chowder, 62
Salsa, guacamole, 41
Sauces:
  autumntime applesauce, 231
  cranberry-pear-walnut, 185
  eggnog, 191
  Italian green herb, 93
  mint-apple, 231
  Moroccan hot, 151
  see also Condiments
Sauerbraten, Erna's, 132–133

Sauerkraut, 114
  and sausage casserole Alsace,
    114
Sausage:
  frijoles gorditos, 76–77
  and kale soup, Portuguese, 48
  and lentil stew, 75
  and pork cazuela, 102–103
  Ricardo's chile con queso, 17
  and sauerkraut casserole Al-
    sace, 114
  scallop, and shrimp jam-
    balaya, 70
  Thanksgiving stuffing, 181
Scallop(s):
  chowder, Big Apple, 61
  North Beach cioppino, 65
  seafood etouffé, 64
  shrimp, and sausage jam-
    balaya, 70
Scalloped summer squash, 173
Seafood, 59–70
  Athenian shrimp in tomato
    and feta sauce, 63
  Big Apple scallop chowder, 61
  etouffé, 64
  farmers' market lobster and
    corn chowder, 69
  Nor'eastern shrimp chowder,
    60
  North Beach cioppino, 65
  salmon, mushroom, and pea
    chowder, 62
  scallop, shrimp, and sausage
    jambalaya, 70
  snapper, oyster, and ham
    gumbo, 68
  soupe de poissons, 66–67
  turkey breast tonnato, 159
  white bean, tuna, and tomato
    salad, 83

Shellfish, see Seafood
Shepherd's stew, 109
Short ribs with garden patch
  horseradish sauce, 98
Shrimp:
  chowder, Nor'eastern, 60
  North Beach cioppino, 65
  scallop, and sausage jam-
    balaya, 70
  seafood etouffé, 64
  slow-cooked paella, 155
  in tomato and feta sauce,
    Athenian, 63
Side dishes, 163–185
  cranberry-pear-walnut sauce,
    185
  gingered apple butter, 183
  herbed Thanksgiving stuffing,
    180–181
  pineapple and macadamia
    chutney, 184–185
  wild rice, apricot, and pecan
    dressing, 182
  see also Go-withs; Vegetable
    side dishes
Slaw, Chinese cabbage and peanut, 227
Snapper, red:
  North Beach cioppino, 65
  oyster, and ham gumbo, 68
  soupe de poissons, 66–67
Soupe de poissons, 66–67
Soups, 27–52
  Amish country chicken "pot
    pie," 147
  beef goulash pot, 38
  beefy borscht, 32–33
  Big Apple scallop chowder,
    61
  black bean and smoked tur-
    key, 45